DICKENS AND YOUTH

Also by Frank Donovan

The Medal
The Tall Frigates
The Early Eagles
The Unlucky Hero
The Americanism of Barry Goldwater
Wheels for a Nation
The Women in Their Lives
Riverboats of America
Mr. Monroe's Message
Mr. Lincoln's Proclamation
Mr. Madison's Constitution
Mr. Roosevelt's Four Freedoms
Mr. Jefferson's Declaration

THE PAPERS OF THE FOUNDING FATHERS

The Benjamin Franklin Papers
The Thomas Jefferson Papers
The George Washington Papers
The John Adams Papers

JUVENILES

The Ironclads
The Brave Traitor
The Cutter
The Many Worlds of Benjamin Franklin
Famous Twentieth Century Leaders
Ironclads of the Civil War
The Vikings

DICKENS
and YOUTH

By FRANK DONOVAN

ILLUSTRATED

DODD, MEAD & COMPANY

NEW YORK

Library of Congress Catalog Card Number: 68-8281
Printed in the United States of America
by The Cornwall Press, Inc., Cornwall, N. Y.

CONTENTS

ILLUSTRATIONS

DICKENS AND YOUTH

CHAPTER

I

~~~

THE VISION OF THE CHILD

"There was once a child, and he strolled about a good deal, and thought about a number of things. He had a sister, who was a child too, and his constant companion. These two used to wonder all day long. They wondered at the beauty of the flowers; they wondered at the height and blueness of the sky; they wondered at the depth of the bright water; they wondered at the goodness and the power of God, who made the lovely world.

"They used to say to one another, sometimes, supposing all the children upon earth were to die, would the flowers and the water and the sky be sorry? They believed that they would be sorry. For, said they, the buds are the children of the flowers, and the little playful streams that gambol down the hillsides are the children of the water; and the smallest bright specks playing hide and seek in the sky all night, must surely be the children of the stars; and they would all be grieved to see their playmates, the children of men, no more."

Surely these lines from Dickens' *Child's Dream of a Star* are part of what the eminent Dickensian W. Walter Crotch meant when he wrote that Charles Dickens had "the vision of the child"—a deep understanding of youth, of the minds, motivations, the characters and consciences of children and adolescents.

Dickens saw the lost world of childhood in a romantic, almost mystical, light. To him childhood was a dream of perfect life when, he wrote, "everything was happy, when there was no distance and no time." It was "the best and purest link between this world and a better." The fascination, he said, was one he "did not care to resist," and in his writings he fondly recalled "the old green field with its gently waving trees, where the birds sang as he had never heard since—when butterflies fluttered far more gaily than he ever sees them now, in all his ramblings—when the sky seemed bluer, and the sun shone more brightly—when the air blew more freshly over greener grass, and sweeter-smelling flowers—where everything wore a richer and more brilliant hue than it is ever dressed in now."

Dickens' multifarious interests prompted him to write about many things, but through all his work there marches a cast of juvenile characters unique in the world of literature. No other author wrote so extensively about youth in all its aspects. Said Crotch: "The Pied Piper himself was not followed by a larger, noisier, jollier, or a more motley crowd of youngsters than those which sprang teeming from the creative brain of Dickens." From the Boz sketches, which were Dickens' first published work, to *Our Mutual Friend*, covering a period of thirty years in his career, young people played a part in almost everything he wrote—sometimes incidently, more frequently as leading or principal characters, as in *David*

Copperfield, *Oliver Twist*, *Old Curiosity Shop*, *Dombey and Son*, and several more.

Dickens was the first English novelist in whose stories children and young people played central parts. In fact, he was virtually the first to introduce children into English literature. Prior to Dickens there were a few incidental juveniles in the writing of Sir Walter Scott, a chapter or so in *Tristram Shandy*, and a couple of incredible schoolgirls by Jane Austen. Of Dickens' fifteen novels (including *Pickwick Papers*, which some do not classify as a novel), only four failed to give a prominent place to children, and there are many more juvenile characters in his shorter Christmas stories and magazine pieces and in the reportorial vignettes of his early writings. After his death, in the Memorial Sermon at Westminster Abbey, Dean Stanley referred to the "lesson" taught by the stories of Oliver Twist, Tiny Tim in *Christmas Carol*, and Little Nell in *Old Curiosity Shop* and said that the grave of Dickens would "seem to those who crowd around it as though it were the very grave of those innocents whom he had thus created for our companionship, for our instruction, for our delight and solace."

On his initial trip to America, in 1842, the novelist thanked his first audience for the many letters about Little Nell that he had received "from the dwellers in log-houses among the morasses, and swamps, and densest forest, and deepest solitudes of the Far West." Little Nell, and the other "rejected ones whom the world has too long forgotten, and too often misused," had formed a bond between him and his public. "At every act of kindness on your part," he continued, "I say to myself, 'that's for Oliver; I should not wonder if that were meant for Smike [a boy in *Nicholas Nickleby*]; I have no doubt that is intended for Nell.'"

Dickens was interested in youth because he was interested in life, and life starts with youth. He championed youth because he was a revolutionary and endorsed the demand of youth for change. "It will easily be believed," he wrote, "that I am a fond parent to every child of my fancy, and that no one can ever love that family as dearly as I love them." He favored youth because he was a reformer, and youth provided him with subjects for his crusades. There are many evidences of this throughout his writings, and two novels are devoted primarily to exposing wrongs to children—the poorhouse system in *Oliver Twist* and the cheap public schools in *Nicholas Nickleby*. In *Great Expectations* he wrote, "In the little world in which children have their existence, whosoever brings them up, there is nothing so fiercely perceived and so finely felt as injustice. It may only be a small injustice that the child is exposed to; but the child is small, and its world is small."

Before he was a novelist Dickens was a reporter, engaged in a craft to which he brought a brilliant talent which he never lost throughout his life. He applied his reporting skill to his crusading reforms and interpreted the result in fiction for, he said, "fictitious narratives place the enormities of the system in a much stronger point of view." His reporter's eye sharply noted facts and places and people which his novelist's imagination transformed into emotional flesh and blood. He visited the mills of Manchester to observe at first hand the evils of child labor and after his inspection wrote: "What I have seen has disgusted me and astonished me beyond all measure. I intend to strike the heaviest blow in my power for these unfortunate creatures, but whether I shall do so in 'Nickleby' or wait some other opportunity, I have not yet determined."

Most of Dickens' juvenile characters started in the eye of

the reporter. They are romantic caricatures of real young-sters. Their actions and motivations have a sound basis in actual juvenile thought and behavior. He took great pride in the lifelikeness of his portrayals of youth. When his friend and earliest biographer, John Forster, commented on a portion of *Oliver Twist* while it was being written, Dickens hastened to reply: "How can I thank you? Can I do better than by saying that the sense of poor Oliver's reality, which I know you have had from the first, has been the highest of all praise to me? None that has been lavished upon me have I felt half so much."

Dickens' children were lifelike because he liked and respected the originals, including his own nine offspring. "It would be difficult," he wrote, "to overstate the intensity and accuracy of an intelligent child's observation." Said one critic: "The boundless affection of Dickens for his little creations, bearing the scars and wounds of an unheeding world of strife, is such that he made us behold them in their simple griefs as well as their juvenile joys."

Dickens' earliest youngsters appeared in *Sketches by Boz*, a series of short pieces which he started to write when he was twenty-one years old and which first appeared, without compensation to the author, in the "Monthly Magazine." The pseudonym Boz with which his early work was signed arose from a jesting nickname for his seven-year-old brother, "whom in honor of the *Vicar of Wakefield* he had dubbed Moses." The child's nasal mispronunciation of Moses as "Boses" was shortened to "Bose" and finally became "Boz" by the time Dickens borrowed it. The sketches were of two categories. Most were reports on scenes and places and people and pieces of action which attracted the writer as he roamed the streets of London. Others were more imaginative vignettes of incidents or happenings developed from reality. One of the former classification described "The Streets—Morning" and the people who were to be seen as London came awake, including:

"Small office boys in large hats, who are made men before they are boys, hurry along in pairs, with their first coat carefully brushed, and the white trousers of last Sunday plentifully besmeared with ink. It evidently requires a considerable mental struggle to avoid investing part of the day's dinner-money in the purchase of the stale tarts so temptingly exposed in dusty tins at the pastry-cooks' doors; but a consciousness of their own importance, and the receipt of seven shillings a week, with the prospect of an early rise to eight, comes to their aid, and they accordingly put their hats a little more to one side, and look under the bonnets of all the milliners' and staymakers' apprentices they meet—poor girls!—the hardest worked, the worst paid, and too often, the worst used class of the community."

Most memorable of the *Sketches by Boz* are those dealing with the seamy side of life. Dickens was, then and later, dedicated to bringing to light the wretched conditions of the poor, which were responsible for crime and immorality to which youth succumbed. He haunted the courts and the prisons, reporting scenes of youthful misery. In a sketch titled "Criminal Courts," he described "an elderly woman, of decent appearance, though evidently poor, and a boy of about fourteen or fifteen." The woman had come to get her son when he was released.

"We cannot forget the boy; he descended the stairs with a dogged look, shaking his head with an air of bravado and obstinate determination. They walked a few paces, and paused. The woman put her hand on his shoulder in an agony

of entreaty, and the boy sullenly raised his head as if in refusal. It was a brilliant morning, and every object looked
fresh and happy in the broad, gay sunlight; he gazed round
him for a few moments, bewildered with the brightness of the
scene, for it was a long time since he had beheld anything
save the gloomy walls of a prison. Perhaps the wretchedness
of his mother made some impression on the boy's heart; perhaps some undefined recollection of the time when he was a
happy child, and she his only friend and best companion,
crowded on him—he burst into tears; and covering his face
with his hand, and hurriedly placing the other in his mother's,
walked away with her."

In "A Visit to Newgate" Dickens wrote a companion piece
of a teen-aged girl whom he observed in the prison. "The girl
belonged to a class—unhappily but too extensive—the very
existence of which should make men's hearts bleed. Barely
past her childhood, it requires but a glance to discover that
she was one of those children, born and bred in neglect and
vice, who have never known what childhood is; who have
never been taught to love and court a parent's smile, or to
dread a parent's frown. The thousand nameless endearments
of childhood, its gaiety and its innocence, are alike unknown
to them. They have entered at once upon the stern realities
and miseries of life, and to their better nature it is almost
hopeless to appeal in after-times, by any of the references
which will awaken, if only for a moment, some good feeling
in ordinary bosoms, however corrupt they may have become.
Talk to *them* of parental solicitude, the happy days of childhood, and the merry games of infancy! Tell them of hunger
and the streets, beggary and stripes, the gin-shop, the station-
house, and the pawn-broker's and they will understand you."

In one of the shortest of the Boz sketches, "The Prisoner's

Van," Dickens delineates a type of juvenile character that always aroused his interest and his pity—the teen-age prostitute. Those whom he saw in the streets of London in real life he later placed in novels as fictional characters—Martha Endell in *David Copperfield* and Nancy in *Oliver Twist*. "The Prisoner's Van" starts with a description of the callous crowd that presses around the door of the police station, waiting for the prisoners to be put in the van that will take them to jail. As the van draws up "the people thronged around the steps, leaving a little alley for the prisoners to pass through. . . .

"After a few minutes' delay, the door again opened, and the two first prisoners appeared. They were a couple of girls, of whom the elder could not have been more than sixteen, and the younger of whom certainly had not attained her fourteenth year. That they were sisters was evident from the resemblance which still subsisted between them, though two additional years of depravity had fixed their brand upon the elder girl's features, as legibly as if a red-hot iron had seared them. They were both gaudily dressed, the younger one especially; and, although there was a strong similarity between them in both respects, which was rendered the more obvious by their being handcuffed together, it is impossible to conceive a greater contrast than the demeanor of the two presented. The younger girl was weeping bitterly—not for display, or in the hope of producing effect, but for very shame; her face was buried in her handkerchief: and her whole manner was but too expressive of bitter and unavailing sorrow.

" 'How long are you in for, Emily?' screamed a red-faced woman in the crowd. 'Six weeks and labour,' replied the elder girl with a flaunting laugh; 'and that's better than the stone jug anyhow; the mill's a better deal than the Sessions, and here's Bella a-going too for the first time. Hold up your head, you chicken,' she continued, boisterously tearing the other girl's handkerchief away; 'Hold up your head and show 'em your face. I an't jealous, but I'm blessed if I an't game!' 'That's right, old gal,' exclaimed a man in a paper cap, who in common with the greater part of the crowd had been inexpressibly delighted with this little incident. —'Right!' replied the girl; 'ah, to be sure; what's the odds, eh?'—'Come! in with you,' interrupted the driver. 'Don't you be in a hurry, coachman,' replied the girl, 'and recollect I want to be set down in Cold Bath Fields—large house with a high garden-wall in front; you can't mistake it. Hallo! Bella, where are you going to—you'll pull my precious arm off!' This was addressed to the younger girl, who, in her anxiety to hide herself in the caravan, had ascended the steps first and forgotten the strain upon the handcuff. 'Come down and let's show you the way.' And after jerking the miserable girl down with a force which made her stagger on the pavement, she got into the vehicle and was followed by her wretched companion.

"These two girls had been thrown upon London streets, their vices and debauchery, by a rapacious mother. What the younger girl was then, the elder had been once; and what the elder then was, the younger must soon become. A melancholy prospect, but how surely to be realized; a tragic drama, but how often acted!"

Dickens' fictional fallen girls, like their creator, had a dreadful fascination with the river—the dark, moody, dirty Thames that flowed through London along whose banks the youthful Dickens roamed. Nancy in *Oliver Twist* and Little Em'ly in *David Copperfield* both talk of ending their shame in the river, and Martha Endell in the latter book tried to drown herself, seeing a parallel between her own life and the river.

"Oh, the river! The river! . . . I know it's like me. I know that I belong to it. I know that it's the natural company for such as I am. It comes from country places, where there was once no harm in it—and it creeps through the dismal streets, defiled and miserable. . . . I can't keep away from it. I can't forget it. It haunts me day and night. It's the only thing in all the world that I am fit for, or that's fit for me. Oh, the dreadful river."

Dickens did not confine his interest in fallen girls to reporting and fiction. He was instrumental in establishing a home where such unfortunate young women could be rehabilitated and for a time assisted in the management of it. He influenced a wealthy friend, Baroness Burdett-Coutts, to finance Urania Cottage where girls who had been convicted of prostitution might go after their release from prison. "I would put it in the power of any penitent creature to knock at the door, and say for God's sake, take me in." He chose the house, selected the matron, took pains to find out all that he could about the past lives of the girls, drew up the plan under which the girls were to be led back to a better life, and wrote an appeal to the girls offering them shelter in the home.

This latter was a circular letter that was delivered, at the discretion of the wardens, to girls in prison for whom there seemed to be some hope of regeneration. This was sound psychology; it caught the girl when she was at a low point and when a change in her way of life might seem most attractive. It started: "You will see, on beginning to read this letter, that it is not addressed to you by name. But I address it to a woman—a very young woman still—who was born to be happy, and has lived miserably; who has no prospect before her but sorrow, or behind her but a wasted youth." The letter continued to say that there was now a chance for the girl to have a quiet home, friends, self-respect, peace of mind—"Not a chance but the *certainty* of all these blessings, if you will exert yourself to deserve them." Dickens then painted, with his inimitable skill, the life of a girl of the streets as he had observed it and a projection of that life into the future:

"You know what the streets are; you know how cruel the companions that you find there are; you know the vices practiced there and to what wretched consequences they bring you, even while you are young. Shunned by decent people, marked out by all other kinds of women as you walk along, avoided by the very children, hunted by the police, imprisoned, and only set free to be imprisoned over and over again —reading this very letter in a common goal—you have, already, dismal experience of the truth. But, to grow old in such a way of life, and among such company—to escape an early death from terrible disease, or from your own maddened hand, and arrive at an old age in such a course—will be an aggravation of every misery that you know now, which words cannot describe. Imagine for yourself the bed on which you, then an object terrible to look at, will lie down to die. Imagine all the long, long years of shame, want, crime, and ruin, that will rise before you. And by that dreadful day, and by the Judgment that will follow it, and by the recollection that you are certain to have then, when it is too late, of the offer that is made to you now, when it is NOT too late, I implore you to think of it, and weigh it well!"

Dickensians have long argued and speculated about the extent to which Dickens' juvenile characters and incidents in their fictional lives were autobiographical. It is certainly true that much of the first quarter of *David Copperfield* paralleled the life of its creator, and the characters of many of his other boy heroes were influenced by his own life experiences. Late in life he wrote a series of personal essays, often reminiscent in tone, which first appeared in a magazine that he edited, "All The Year Round," collectively titled *The Uncommercial Traveller*. Some of these that deal with childhood contain fragments of autobiography. In one, which he called "Dullborough Town," Dickens returned in imagination to Chatham where he had lived as a child. "As I left Dullborough in the days when there were no railroads in the land, I left it in a stage-coach. Through all the years that have since passed, have I ever lost the smell of the damp straw in which I was packed—like game—and forwarded, carriage paid, to the Cross Keys, Wood Street, Cheapside, London? With this tender remembrance upon me, I was cavalierly shunted back into Dullborough the other day, by train."

He found that much had changed. The station had swallowed up the playing field where, ". . . in haymaking time, had I been delivered from the dungeons of Seringapatam, an immense pile (of haycock), by my countrymen, the victorious British (boy next door and his two cousins), and had been recognized with extasy by my affianced one (Miss Green), who had come all the way from England (second house in the terrace) to ransom me, and marry me. Here, had I first heard in confidence, from one whose father was greatly connected, being under Government, of the existence of a terrible banditti, called 'The Radicals,' whose principles were, that the Prince Regent wore stays, and that nobody had a right to any salary, and that the army and navy ought to be put down—horrors at which I trembled in my bed, after supplicating that the Radicals might be speedily taken and hanged."

He also recalled that ". . . in my very young days I was taken to so many lyings-in that I wonder I escaped becoming

a professional martyr to them in after-life. I suppose I had a
very sympathetic nurse, with a large circle of married acquaintance. However that was, as I continued my walk
through Dullborough, I found many houses to be solely
associated in my mind with this particular interest. At one
little greengrocer's shop, down certain steps from the street, I
remembered to have waited on a lady who had four children
(I am afraid to write five, though I fully believe it was five)
at a birth. This meritorious woman held quite a Reception in
her room in the morning when I was introduced there, and
the sight of the house brought vividly to my mind how the
four (five) deceased young people lay, side by side, on a
clean cloth on a chest of drawers: reminding me by a homely
association, which I suspect their complexion to have assisted,
of pigs' feet as they are usually displayed at a neat tripe-shop."

In "Birthday Celebrations," another of *The Uncommercial
Traveller* sketches, Dickens recalled several anniversaries between his tender years and the attainment of his majority. Of
the first he wrote: "I can very well remember being taken out
to visit some peach-faced creature in a blue sash, and shoes to
correspond, whose life I supposed to consist entirely of birthdays. Upon seed-cake, sweet wine, and shining presents, that
glorified young person seemed to me to be exclusively reared.
At so early a stage of my travels did I assist at the anniversary
of her nativity (and become enamored of her), that I had not
yet acquired the recondite knowledge that a birthday is the
common property of all who are born, but supposed it to be a
special gift bestowed by the favoring heavens on that one
distinguished infant. There was no other company, and we
sat in a shady bower—under a table, as my better (or worse)
knowledge leads me to believe—and were regaled with sac-
charine substances and liquids, until it was time to part. A bit-

ter powder was administered to me next morning, and I was wretched. On the whole, a pretty accurate foreshadowing of my more mature experiences in such wise!"

A schoolmaster was recalled in *The Uncommercial Traveller*, a certain Mr. Barlow, although there is no record of a pedagogue by that name in Dickens' life. Whoever this instructor was he earned Dickens' lifelong ill will by his unfortunate debunking of the products of the novelist's imagination. Dickens asked: "What right had he to bore his way into my Arabian Nights? Yet he did. He was always hinting doubts of the veracity of Sinbad the Sailor. If he could have got hold of the Wonderful Lamp, I knew he would have trimmed it and lighted it, and delivered a lecture over it on the qualities of sperm oil, with a glance at the whale fisheries . . . He would have proved, by map and compass, that there was no such kingdom of Casgar, on the frontiers of Tartary."

There is great paradox involving Dickens' fictional children. In discussing childhood, as such, he always presented it as the most desirable stage of life—a time when "everything was happy." His works are replete with descriptions of gay children playing in an ideal, natural atmosphere, free from the cares and problems of the adult world and far from the unwholesome aspects of the squalid city. Typical of such an idyl is a passage from *Nicholas Nickleby* where Nicholas takes the dying Smike into the countryside and the boy reminisces about his youth in these delightful surroundings: "With what longing and enjoyment he would point out some tree that he had climbed a hundred times to peep at the birds in their nests, and then the branch from which he used to shout to little Kate, who stood below terrified. There is the old house with the tiny window through which the sun used to stream in and wake him in the summer mornings—

they were all summer mornings then—and the very rosebush, a present from some little lover, and which she had planted with her own hands. There were the hedgerows in which they had so often gathered wild flowers together—it all came back upon the mind, as events of childhood do. Nothing in itself—perhaps a word, a laugh, a look, but better than the hardest words or severest sorrows of eye."

But when Dickens describes such a childhood it is usually in terms of something long lost, or something that might have been. Smike, when the reader first meets him, is in a bleak Yorkshire school where the lives of the students are a constant misery. Despite his emphasis on the happiness of childhood, it is hard to find a happy child in Dickens. The one adjective that applies to almost all of them is pathetic. Several of his child characters meet early deaths, some of them are cripples or otherwise shortchanged by nature. Those that are whole and live are usually buffeted in one way or another by the ill winds of fate. A very high percentage are orphans or half-orphans and are denied the stability of a loving home. Dickens wrote extensively about the charms of hearth and home, but with few exceptions—the Toodles children in *Dombey and Son*, the Cratchit youngsters in the *Christmas Carol*, the Kenwigs children in *Nicholas Nickleby*, and one or two others—none of his youngsters have such a home. Most of his children are maltreated, subject to sarcasm, bad temper, and restrictive convictions of parents or guardians—when they are not whipped, beaten, or kept in solitary confinement. Dickens extolls the charms of the country, but his little heroes and heroines are mostly left longing for such charms while they live their weary lives in the fetid streets, moldy dwellings, workhouses, or suppressive schools.

The bulk of the children are poor and of the lower class.

Many were children of the London streets, surrounded by vice and filth, cruelty and neglect. The heart of Dickens the reformer was with such children; these were the youngsters who most needed the type of childhood which he eulogized when he wrote about childhood rather than children. Dickens understood such waifs—G. K. Chesterton summarized his grasp of the creatures of the slums by saying that Dickens had "the key to the street."

The orphans or half-orphans in Dickens' writing form an impressive list. Oliver Twist is an orphan, as are Noah Claypole and Fagin's band of young pickpockets in that book. Pip in *Great Expectations* is an orphan, as are Martin Chuzzlewit and Little Nell. In *David Copperfield* there are four juvenile orphans—Emily, Traddles, the Orfling, and Martha Endell—and six half-orphans; Dora and Agnes have no mother, and Heep, Ham, Steerforth, and David himself have no father. Barnaby Rudge is abandoned by his murdering father. The mother of the Dombey children dies at Paul's birth. Little Dorrit's mother dies when she is eight. *Nicholas Nickleby* starts with the death of the hero's father, and the mother of Madeline Bray in that novel, dies when Madeline is a young child. Kit Nubbles, Little Nell's admirer in *Old Curiosity Shop,* is another fatherless child, and in that same book Dick Swiveller cries out: "Left an infant by my parents at an early age . . . cast upon the world in my tenderest periods . . . Here's a miserable orphan for you."

Many of Dickens' children who are not orphaned are in a worse state because of cruel, neglectful, rejective, or oppressive parents, or surrogate parents, usually in the form of schoolmasters or schoolmistresses. In *Dombey and Son* he wrote: "Not an orphan in the world can be so deserted as the child who is an outcast from a living parent's love." In that book there are three parents who signally fail to discharge their responsibilities; in *Barnaby Rudge* there are five. One review of *Little Dorrit* commented on the "remarkable number of false and inadequate parents." *Nicholas Nickleby* is peopled entirely by unwanted children, "one huge indictment of the failure of parental responsibility." In one letter Dickens wrote that the greater number of parents who came under his observation seemed to him to be selfish in their behavior to their children.

To most of his children the adult world is vicious, hostile, uncomprehending, or indifferent. Typical of the parental background against which many of his children were raised is the recollection of Arthur Clennam in *Little Dorrit* of his upbringing: "Trained by main force; broken, not bent . . . I am the child of parents who weighed, measured, and priced everything . . . Austere faces, inexorable discipline, pennance in this world and terror in the next—nothing graceful or gentle anywhere, and the void in my cowed heart everywhere—this was my childhood, if I may so misuse the word as to apply it to such a beginning of life."

Many of Dickens' fictional children who were not mistreated were often misunderstood. In a late essay he discoursed on the ill effects of not paying attention to childish beliefs and fancies: "It would be difficult to overstate the intensity and accuracy of an intelligent child's observation. At that impressible time of life, it must sometimes produce a fixed impression. If the fixed impression be of an object terrible to the child, it will be (for want of reasoning upon) inseparable from great fear. Force the child at such a time, be Spartan with it, send it into the dark against its will, leave it in a lonely bedroom against its will, and you had better murder it."

Dickens had ideas on child-rearing that were far in advance of his time. A modern child psychologist would heartily approve the sentiments of the above quotation, which Dickens pointed up in several novels by instances of the cruelty of "forcing" a child or ignoring its "silly" beliefs. In *Dombey and Son* Mrs. Pipchin would stand no nonsense from her little charges and used Spartan methods to correct it: "As little Miss Pankey was afraid of sleeping alone in the dark, Mrs. Pipchin always made it a point of driving her upstairs herself, like a sheep; and it was cheerful to hear Miss Pankey moaning long afterwards, in the least eligible chamber, and Mrs. Pipchin now and then going in to shake her."

Most of Dickens' children are lonely as well as neglected. Few had brothers or sisters and most of his heroes had no friends. Deprived of parental love, many of the youngsters were thrust out into an alien adult world to fend for themselves. Typical of the situation in which many Dickens' children found themselves is this description of Oliver Twist's feelings when he is captured by Fagin's minions: "Weak with recent illness; stupefied by the blows and the suddenness of the attack; terrified by the fierce growling of the dog, and the brutality of the man, over-powered by the conviction of the bystanders that he really was the hardened little wretch he was described to be; what could one poor child do? Darkness had set in; it was a low neighborhood; no help was near; resistance was useless. In another moment, he was dragged into a labyrinth of dark, narrow courts." "*What could one poor child do*" might be termed a slogan of the Dickens' child.

Analysts of the psychology of Dickens trace his preoccupation with neglected and rejected children to his belief that he was himself the victim of parental neglect and rejection. In a letter to Nathaniel Hawthorne he described himself as "a very

small and not-overparticularly-taken-care-of-boy." Throughout his life he resented the fact that he had not been given an
education. For this he blamed his father. His male parent was,
he said, "as kind-hearted and generous a man as ever lived in
the world." But, he added, "In the ease of his temper and the
straitness of his means, he appeared to have utterly lost at this
time the idea of educating me at all, and to have utterly put
from him the notion that I had any claim upon him, in that
regard whatever. So I degenerated into cleaning his boots of
a morning, and my own; and making myself useful in the
work of the little house; and looking after my younger
brothers and sisters; and going on such poor errands as arose
out of our poor way of living."

Dickens considered his mother rejective mainly because of
an incident in his twelfth year. He had been placed to work
in a blacking warehouse, a situation which filled him with
humiliation and bitterness. When he was discharged as a result
of a disagreement between his father and his employer, his
mother intervened and induced the employer to offer to take
him back. His father refused and sent the boy belatedly to
school. Many years later Dickens wrote: "I never afterwards
forgot, I never shall forget, I never can forget, that my
mother was warm for my being sent back." In general,
Dickens seemed to consider his mother as rather silly and created a caricature of her in Mrs. Nickleby, who was a rather
stupid woman "who had at no time been remarkable for the
possession of a very clear understanding."

Dickens also said of himself that "he always was a puny,
weak youngster" prone to "violent spasmodic attacks, which
used to utterly prostrate him." The active games of boys "had
no charm for him, save such as lay in watching others play."
Active games and sports had no charms for his young heroes

either. Steerforth in *David Copperfield* is the only one who shows even a casual interest in athletic pursuits. There is little external evidence to support Dickens' picture of himself as a physically weak, rejected child, but there is no question that he had a great fund of self-pity for his lost, neglected childhood, which motivated his pleas for the rights of youth. He saw himself as a Paul Dombey who, unlike the fictional child, had survived to adulthood and he identified with many of his forlorn juvenile characters.

Identification was also responsible for a whole group of Dickens' heroines. He had a peculiar affection for a strange kind of little girl, one with a sort of saintly precocity. Agnes Wickford in *David Copperfield* was one such, as was Rose Maylie in *Oliver Twist*. Florence Dombey and Madeline Bray were others. Of Little Dorrit he said that goodness shone forth from her "pale, transparent face," and Little Nell was "a creature fresh from the hand of God." These girls were not children—they were little mothers even in their tender years. They were the embodiment of innocence—virginal, ethereal, and essentially sexless.

Most Dickensians believe that the saintly girls were based on the memory of the author's sister-in-law, Mary Hogarth, who at the age of sixteen came to live with Dickens and his wife shortly after their marriage and who died when she was seventeen. Dickens loved Mary so deeply that he wanted to share her grave. There was never a hint of the conventional (or unconventional) *ménage au trois* in his relationship with Mary, although his wife, Kate, could never live up to her husband's concept of womanhood as exemplified by her younger sister. Of Dickens' feeling for his sister-in-law, Professor Johnson, his most recent biographer, wrote: "It is impossible to exaggerate the significance of this early love and early sorrow for Dickens. His devotion to Mary was an emotion unique in his entire life, not only more enduring and unchanging than any other, but one that touched his being in a way that no other did . . . Mary set in motion in the springs of his imagination a vision of ideal womanhood that was never realized for him again."

In several of his novels Dickens set down this "vision of ideal womanhood" in a progression of heroines that have sometimes been criticized as being too good to be true. They must be accepted as symbols of the antithesis of the forces of evil, the embodiment of supreme good. In her introduction to *Nicholas Nickleby*, Dame Sybil Thorndike wrote: "Though many of his readers feel that Dickens wallows in his Little Nells, his Madeline Brays, and other prototypes in each book, one recognizes that he must have a perfect being to worship (it is nearly always a young girl)—a being who has no vice, no small sins, but is self-sacrificing, helping all who are near her to a realization of what goodness means—the touching even of the hem of a garment bringing healing."

When the story line of a novel required one of these saintly girls to die young, as had Mary, Dickens was thrown into an emotional turmoil. The original plan of *Oliver Twist* called for the death of Rose Maylie, but when the time came Dickens could not bring himself to kill her and wrote another ending. In *Old Curiosity Shop* Little Nell's death could not be avoided, but Dickens postponed writing it. He told the artist who drew the deathbed scene: "I am breaking my heart over this story," and to his friend Forster he said: "I am the wretchedest of the wretched. [The story] casts the most terrible shadow over me, and it is as much as I can do to keep moving at all. I tremble to approach the place . . . Nobody will miss her like I shall. It is such a painful thing to me, that

I really cannot express my sorrow. Old wounds bleed afresh when I only think of the way of doing it. . . . Dear Mary died yesterday, when I think of this sad story."

Numerous children die young in Dickens' novels. The first was "poor little Dick," a workhouse friend of Oliver Twist who was apparently put in the book solely to die, and on his three appearances he talks of nothing else: "I dream so much of Heaven, and angels, and kind faces that I never see when I am awake." The principal juveniles to die were Little Nell, Paul Dombey, Smike in *Nicholas Nickleby* and Dora, David Copperfield's wife. Each of these is the subject of a protracted, highly emotional deathbed scene.

Today these deathbed scenes may seem unduly dramatic and sensational: organ music with all stops out. At the time that Dickens' work was initially published they had great public appeal. Thousands of readers, particularly young girls, literally wept at the death of Little Nell. Writing of Dickens in 1858, Walter Bagehot pointed out that "The unfeeling obtuseness of the early part of this century was to be corrected by an extreme, perhaps an excessive, sensibility to human suffering in the years which have followed."

The juvenile mortality rate was extremely high and deaths of children were described lyrically by clergy and others. Meetings at Ragged Schools featured edifying anecdotes of juvenile deathbeds by the masters, and the obituary of a Ragged School pupil might contain a statement that "Mr. Smith had his reward in a remarkable deathbed scene of one of his pupils." The actual death of a boy in a school in 1838 was described thusly: "The boys were allowed to take a last look at their dying school fellow. The solemn march of the lads across the playground, their tremulous tip-toe tread as they moved around the crib where lay the gasping youth, the

gentle words of solemn warning spoken to the deeply affected and astonished lads, formed a picture of touching interest. All play was by common consent suspended. Well
nigh every boy seemed to be a suppliant at the mercy seat."

CHAPTER

II

DICKENS' FAVORITE CHILD

"Like many fond parents I have in my heart of hearts a favorite child. And his name is David Copperfield." So said
Dickens about the principal character in the book that, well
over a century after it was written in 1849, is still his most
popular work; the one through which most youngsters are
today introduced to the great novelist in school. Of *David
Copperfield* Dickens' most recent biographer, Prof. Edgar
Johnson, wrote: "Few novelists have ever captured more
poignantly the feeling of childhood, the brightness and magic
and terror of the world as seen through the eyes of a child."

Several other Dickens commentators maintain that no other
writer has ever portrayed the life of a child from infancy to
adulthood with the insight and realism of *David Copperfield*.
The story follows David through the boy's early security and
happiness with his childlike mother and the servant Peggotty;
his fear and rejection at the hands of the cold Murdstones; his
hero worship for the older boy Steerforth; his despair and

loneliness in London when he is set to work at an early age; his partial rescue by the Micawbers, and his final haven as a child with the fairy godmother Aunt Betsey. His adolescent trials are likewise very real: his puppy love for Miss Shepherd and the eldest Miss Larkins; his hopeless fight with the butcher's boy; his lack of assurance with the gentleman's gentleman, Littimer; his one instance of rather delightfully delinquent drunken dissipation; the agonies and elation of his love for his child-bride, Dora; his ultimate recognition of Steerforth's corruption—all are things that happen in life as surely as in fiction.

It is not surprising that David's experiences seem real, for David *was* real. He was more than the author's favorite child. The youthful David was, in fact, the boy Charles Dickens. While Dickens lived he gave some autobiographical material on his early years to his friend and first biographer, John Forster. Several of the incidents in *his* life which David Copperfield describes in the first person in the book are taken, almost verbatim, from this material.

But the comparison between the creator and his subject goes deeper than merely remembered incidents. Some experiences that affected Dickens throughout his life are found in the early life of David. Schooling is an example. Dickens, the boy, had hopes of being "distinguished at grammar school and going to Cambridge." This was not to be. With the reversal in his father's fortunes he was forced to work while his parent languished in debtor's prison and his limited formal schooling was deferred until he was in his teens. David, after a brief period in a horrible academy called Salem House, also went to work at an early age while his surrogate father, Mr. Micawber, was in debtor's prison. Later, in his teens, he was sent for some six years to a fine school, where he was outstandingly successful and became the "head boy." This was, perhaps, wishful thinking on the part of his creator. G.K. Chesterton, in his commentary *Charles Dickens, The Last of the Great Men*, made the point that both Dickens and David went "from the world to a school, instead of going from school to the world."

When asked, late in life, about his son's education, John Dickens replied that Charles had educated himself. Dickens described how he did so to Forster almost in these words that he later put in the mouth of David Copperfield: "My father had left a small collection of books in a little room upstairs to which I had access. . . . From that blessed little room, Roderick Random, Peregrine Pickle, Humphrey Clinker, Tom Jones, the Vicar of Wakefield, Gil Blas, and Robinson Crusoe came out, a glorious host, to keep me company. They kept alive my fancy, and my hope of something beyond that place and time,—they, and the *Arabian Nights* and the *Tales of the Genii*—and did me no harm; for whatever harm was in some of them was not there for me. . . . It is curious to me how I could ever have consoled myself under my small troubles (which were great troubles to me) by impersonating my favorite characters in them. . . . I have been Tom Jones (a child's Tom Jones, a harmless creature) for a week together. . . . When I think of it the picture always rises in my mind of a summer evening, the boys at play in the churchyard, and I sitting on my bed, reading as if for life." Said Forster: "Every word of this personal recollection had been written down as fact, some years before it found its way into *David Copperfield*." And both the real Charles and the fictional David were the agents who sold these books and pawned the family possessions, as the fortunes of the real Dickens and the fictional Micawbers declined.

The one experience in Dickens' youth which made the most lasting impression on him was a period of four to six months when, at the age of twelve, he worked pasting labels on pots of shoe blacking in a warehouse. Recent biographers of the "dark Dickens" make much of this childhood trauma and trace its lasting effects on the writer who, in later life, said of this period: "No words can express the secret agony of my soul. . . . The deep remembrance of the sense I had of being utterly neglected and hopeless; of the shame I felt in my position; of the misery it was to my young heart to believe that, day by day, what I had learned, and thought, and delighted in and raised my fancy and emulation up to, was passing away from me, never to be brought back any more, cannot be written."

Dickens had David suffer the same trauma by sending him to work at the age of ten in the warehouse of Murdstone and Grinby, purveyors of wines and spirits. The parallel of the experiences is evident by a comparison of what Dickens wrote in the fragment of autobiography that he gave Forster and in the description of the incident in *David Copperfield*. Of his own entry into Warren's Blacking warehouse he wrote: "It is wonderful to me how I could have been so easily cast away at such an age. It is wonderful to me that, even after my descent into the poor little drudge I had been since we came to London, no one had compassion enough on me—a child of singular abilities, quick, eager, delicate, and soon hurt, bodily and mentally—to suggest that something might have been spared . . . to place me in any common school."

Dickens had David express his emotions in the same situation thusly: "It is a matter of some surprise to me, even now, that I can have been so easily thrown away at such an age. A child of excellent abilities, and with strong powers of obser-

vation, quick, eager, delicate, and soon hurt—bodily or mentally, it seems wonderful to me that nobody should have made
any sign in my behalf. But none was made."

Even the premises in which the real Charles and the fictional
David worked were the same. Dickens described the actual
blacking warehouse as "a crazy, tumble-down old house, abutting of course on the river, and literally overrun with rats. Its
wainscoted rooms, and its rotten floors and staircase, and the
old gray rats swarming down in the cellars, and the sound of
their squeaking and scuffling coming up the stairs at all times
and the dirt and decay of the place rise up visibly before me,
as if I were there again." The warehouse of Murdstone and
Grinby, where David labored, was: "A crazy old house with
a wharf of its own, abutting on the river when the tide was in
and on the mud when the tide was out, and literally overrun
with rats. Its panelled rooms, discolored with the dirt and
smoke of a hundred years, I dare say; its decayed floors and
staircase; the squeaking and scuffling of the old gray rats
down in the cellars; and the dirt and rottenness of the place,
are things, not of many years ago, in my mind, but of the
present instance."

It might be said that Dickens' characterization of the youthful David Copperfield was truly autobiographic in terms of
his response or reaction to the vicissitudes of life, while
David's life experience was more incidently autobiographic.
Unlike his creator, whose parents both lived until he was
grown, David's father had died before he was born and his
mother died before he reached his teens—but not until after
she had married the loathsome Mr. Murdstone who, with his
equally reprehensible maiden sister, was responsible for all the
bitterness of David's preadolescent years.

In the description of the few years before David's stepfather enters the story, Dickens pictures the life of a secure, well-loved child—a security that is really insecure because it is based on a broken home and a weak, ineffectual, and somewhat vain mother. The small David remembers his home as a haven with some frightening aspects—the dark storeroom that is a place to be run past at night because a small boy knows not what dangers may lurk among those "tubs and jars and old tea-chests." The Sunday parlor is rather fearsome, too, after Peggotty tells him of his father's funeral that was held there. When, in that room, his mother reads him the story of Lazarus rising from the dead, he has a nightmare. But there is fun playing around the pigeon house that has no pigeons in it and the great doghouse that has no dog, but only innumerable butterflies, brighter than any butterflies have since been, just as the fruit in the orchard is riper and richer than any fruit of his adult years. Here, too, are things that a youngster's fancy turns into dangerous adversaries: the fowls that look terribly tall and walk in a menacing and ferocious manner and the geese that waddle after him with long necks outstretched. He dreams of these, too, "as a man environed by wild beasts might dream of lions."

The church holds memories. He recalls that there is nothing in later life that is half so green as the grass in that churchyard, nothing half so shady as its trees. He wonders, in the morning when the light strikes the sundial, "Is the sundial glad that it can tell time again?" Inside the edifice is a pulpit that would make a fine castle to play in, with another boy coming up the stairs to attack it, "and having the velvet cushion thrown down on his head." But he knows that he must not play here. He must watch the clergyman at all times, which seems strange because at other times he is told that it is rude to stare, and he is afraid that the minister will stop the service to ask why he is gaping at him. He scans the monumental tablets in the wall and thinks of "Mr. Bodgers, late of this parish"; and what the feelings of Mrs. Bodgers must have been when, "afflictions sore, long time Mr. Bodgers bore, and physicians were in vain." He also wonders how their physician, Dr. Chillip, likes to be reminded once a week that his services were in vain. And so wondering he drops off to sleep and the sturdy Peggotty cradles him in her ample lap.

But David's earliest memories are of his mother and Peggotty. He recalls dancing about the parlor with his mother—the everyday parlor, not the Sunday one—until Clara collapsed for breath in an elbow chair, "winding her bright curls around her fingers and straightening her waist." The child knew, even then, "that she likes to look so well and is proud of being so pretty." The boy thought Peggotty was pretty too, but of a different style of beauty than his mother's, and he confused the good soul mightily when he asked her outright: "You're a very handsome woman, an't you, Peggotty?"

This idyllic period of David's life ends when Peggotty takes him, at the age of eight, to visit her brother Dan, a retired mariner. Several of the principal characters whose lives interact with David's throughout the novel are introduced as children and adolescents, and their early backgrounds and life experiences are developed to establish the motivation for their adult personalities and actions.

The first to be so introduced are Dan Peggotty's burly, simple, good-natured, teen-age nephew, Ham, and a niece David's age, Little Em'ly: ". . . a most beautiful little girl (or I thought her so) with a necklace of blue beads on, who wouldn't let me kiss her when I offered to, but ran away and hid herself." Both Em'ly and Ham are orphans—Em'ly's father had been "drowndead," said Mr. Peggotty. Shy Little

Em'ly was David's childhood love and after they searched for shells beside the sea, David kissed her innocently under the lobster house and told her that he adored her, demanding a like avowal from her, else he would kill himself with a sword. So the days passed; "as if time had not grown up himself yet, but were a child too, and always at play." The fact that both of their fathers had died before they were born is, to David, a special bond between them; but Em'ly is very conscious of a difference. David's father had been a gentleman, his mother a lady, while her parents are simply fisherfolk. The child so wants to be a lady. When she is, she will give Uncle Dan a sky-blue coat with diamond buttons, and other treasures, including a box of money. Being a lady will give her security from the cruel sea that has taken her father, and she can help the poor fishermen with money if the sea hurts them.

In this first introduction of Little Em'ly, Dickens started to lay the groundwork for the tragic melodrama that her life would hold. As the sure-footed girl dashes along the edge of a jetty reaching into the sea, the boy David gives a cry of alarm. The man David, telling the story, recalled "the sudden rashness of the child and her wild look so far off," and sometimes wondered whether, "if the life before her could have been revealed to me at a glance, and so revealed that a child could fully comprehend it, and if her preservation could have depended on a motion of my hand, I ought to have held it up to save her. . . . Would it have been better for Little Em'ly to have the waters close above her head that morning in my sight; and . . . I have answered Yes, it would have been."

David's years of security end with the visit to Mr. Peggotty's. When he returns it is to find his mother married to Mr. Murdstone, whose stern maiden sister is also ensconced in his home. It is soon evident that the Murdstones completely dominate the weak Clara. Peggotty is banished to the kitchen, where servants belong. David is moved from his well-loved room to a more remote one. Outdoors, a large black dog that barked at him has replaced the bright butterflies in the deserted doghouse. Mr. Murdstone soon makes clear what David is to expect by telling how he handles an obstinate horse or dog. "I beat him . . . I make him wince and smart. I say to myself: 'I'll conquer that fellow'; and if it were to cost him all the blood he had, I should do it."

David might have been made "another creature for life" by a kind word at that time: "a word of encouragement and explanation, of pity for my childish ignorance, of welcome home, of reassurance that it *was* my home, might have made me dutiful to him in my heart, instead of in my hypocritical outside." But there is no word of kindness. His relationship with his stepfather comes to a critical head at the end of some six months when Mr. Murdstone beats the lad with a "lithe and limber" cane because he could not do the lessons which his mother sought to teach him—a fault caused by the silent, disapproving supervision of the Murdstones of the daily teaching period. With his head locked as in a vise under his tormentor's arm, the terrified David, as the cane descends, twists to catch Mr. Murdstone's hand between his teeth and bites it through.

This leads to the banishment of the boy to Salem Hall, a disreputable academy of the type that Dickens had exposed in his previous novel, *Nicholas Nickleby*. It is a "forlorn and desolate" place that smelled like "mildewed corduroys, sweet apples wanting air, and rotten books." Here David is at first compelled to wear on his back, by instruction of Mr. Murdstone, a placard that proclaims: "Take care of him. He bites," a circumstance that causes many tears on David's part when the other boys call him Towzer and command him to "lie down" and that leads to repeated nightmares in which the unhappy eight-year-old makes people scream and stare by running through the streets with nothing on but his night-shirt and the placard.

Ogre of Salem Hall is the headmaster, Mr. Creakle, than whom no man ever enjoyed his profession more, for he has "a delight in cutting at the boys, which was like the satisfaction of a craving appetite." As Mr. Creakle prowls the aisles David sits at his desk pretending to work but secretly watching his eye, morbidly attracted to it, "in a dread desire to know what he will do next, and whether it will be my turn to suffer, or somebody else's." When a culprit is found guilty of an im-perfect exercise, Mr. Creakle cuts a joke before he beats him, "and we laugh at it—miserable little dogs, we laugh, with our visages as white as ashes, and our hearts sinking into our boots."

In Salem Hall David meets two more of the juvenile char-acters who will maintain prominent places in his life story. The first is Tommy Traddles, a good-natured, merry, friendly boy, "in a tight sky-blue suit that made his arms and legs like German sausages, or roly-poly puddings." Because he is merry, and because he is too honorable to snitch on the other boys, even if it means taking punishment itself, Trad-dles is a frequent victim of Mr. Creakle's: "I think he was caned every day that half-year, except one holiday Monday when he was only rulered on both hands." Tommy weeps copiously at such beatings, but soon laughs through his tears and covers his slate with drawings of his favorite—and only—subject, skeletons. David never knew whether Tommy fa-vored skeletons for his art because they were easy "and didn't want any features," or because he was reminded by "those symbols of mortality that caning couldn't last forever."

David's other friend at the school is James Steerforth, a charming, sophisticated, good-looking fourteen-year-old. Because of his manner and his mother's money, Steerforth dominates the meek ushers who serve as teachers and is the only boy whom the tyrannical Mr. Creakle does not dare to strike. Obviously this makes him a hero in the eyes of the other boys, but to none so much as David, whom the older boy befriends —or, rather, from whom he graciously accepts adulation. Modern psychologists explain that such hero worship of an older, glamorous figure is a normal phase of preadolescent development, exaggerated in David's case because he had no other affectionate male figure in his life with whom to identify.

Dickens gives several hints as to Steerforth's true character during his relations with David in Salem House: his supercilious arrogance; his pride, selfishness, and egotism; his need to dominate lesser and weaker figures and to shine in their respectful admiration. The older boy casually suggests that he take care of the little money that David's mother had given him and then induces the neophyte to permit him to squander it on a bedroom feast for the boys—a party at which he graciously condescends to preside, a right which David would not think of questioning, then or later in life, when Steerforth was present. When Steerforth causes the meek usher, Mr. Mell, who has been kind to David, to be discharged, even the most unsophisticated reader begins to see him in his true light. But not David. He is subconsciously aware of the injustice of Steerforth's actions and nothing keeps back his tears except the fear that Steerforth "might think it unfriendly—or, I should say, considering our relative ages and the feelings with which I regarded him, undutiful."

David's stay at Salem House is terminated in less than a year by the death of his mother. Dickens' insight into the innermost mind of a child is evidenced by his description of how David took the news of his mother's death, imparted by Mr. Creakle. The boy is sincerely grief stricken but feels that his affliction confers a kind of dignity upon him. He recalls that, while walking alone in the playground with other boys peeking at him from the windows, "I felt distinguished and looked more melancholy, and walked slower. When school was over and they came and spoke to me, I felt it rather good in myself not to be proud to any of them, and to take exactly the same notice of them all, as before."

David's next experience in life is his brief stint in the warehouse of Murdstone and Grinby—the former a relative of his stepfather's. On a less sensitive child this period would not have been so emotionally catastrophic, but to David, as it had to Dickens himself, it represents the depths of hopelessness; a time when he, like his creator, loses "every hope of growing up to be a learned and distinguished man." The deep resentment and extreme unhappiness of this period for both the real Dickens and the fictional David seems to have been a matter of temperament rather than real hardship. Loneliness was certainly a factor. The other boys in the real and fictional warehouses (one of whom, in David's case, has the engaging name of Mealy Potatoes) try to be friendly, but David seems to feel himself above them socially and intellectually, as had Dickens, who may fairly be called something of a social snob despite his vigorous crusading on behalf of the underprivileged masses. David summarizes this period of his life by recalling: "I know I do not exaggerate, unconsciously and

unintentionally, the scantiness of my resources or the difficulties of my life. . . . I know that I worked from morning
until night, with common men and boys, a shabby child. I
know that I lounged about the streets, insufficiently and un-
satisfactorily fed. I know that, but for the mercy of God, I
might easily have been, for any care that was taken of me, a
little robber or a little vagabond."

But Dickens could not forbear to lighten the story of
David's tribulations by a humorous incident from his own
days in the blacking warehouse. His account in his autobiography and that in *David Copperfield* are almost identical.
In the latter David recalls: "I was such a child, and so little,
that frequently when I went into the bar of a strange public-
house for a glass of ale or porter, to moisten what I had had
for dinner, they were afraid to give it to me. I remember one
hot evening I went into the bar of a public-house and said to
the landlord:

" 'What is your best—your *very* best—ale a glass?' For it
was a special occasion, I don't know what. It may have been
my birthday.

" 'Two pence-halfpenny,' says the landlord, 'is the price
of the Genuine Stunning ale.'

" 'Then,' says I, producing the money, 'just draw me a
glass of the Genuine Stunning, if you please, with a good head
on it.'

"The landlord looked at me in return over the bar, from
head to foot, with a strange smile on his face; and instead of
drawing the beer, looked round the screen and said something
to his wife. She came out from behind it, with her work in
her hand, and joined him in surveying me. Here we stand, all
three, before me now: the landlord in his shirt sleeves, lean-
ing against the bar window-frame; his wife looking over the

little half-door; and I, in some confusion, looking up at them from outside the partition. They asked me a good many questions—as, what my name was, how old I was, where I lived, how was I employed, and how I came there. To all of which, that I might commit nobody, I invented, I am afraid, appropriate answers. They served me with the ale, though I suspect it was not the Genuine Stunning, and the landlord's wife, opening the little half-door of the bar, and bending down, gave me my money back, and gave me a kiss that was half admiring, and half compassionate, but all womanly and good, I am sure."

David's stint at Murdstone and Grinby's has one compensation. On his first day there he meets Wilkens Micawber, one of Dickens' most memorable characters. Mr. Micawber was, at the time, an itinerant commission salesman for the wine merchants—who seldom made any commissions. He takes David to lodge in his home with his wife and four small children; including infant twins, one or the other of whom is constantly nursing at Mrs. Micawber's breast. Another member of the household is a child servant girl from an orphanage —the "Orfling" who was also a real life character from Dickens' boyhood, an orphan servant girl in his own home. The writer did little with the Orfling in *David Copperfield*. He had already developed the same original more fully as the sharp-witted and kindly servant girl, the Marchioness, in *Old Curiosity Shop*.

Wilkens Micawber was John Dickens, Charles's father. Both were pompous, kindly, and well-meaning men. Neither was lazy or indolent, but they had a common fault—they were irresponsible in their handling of money. For this the real John Dickens spent three months in Marshalsea prison where the boy Charles visited him regularly; an experience that he developed more fully, fictionally, in *Little Dorrit* than in *David Copperfield*. Mr. Micawber spends a like period in Fleet Street prison, where the boy David visits him. In the character of Micawber, Dickens copied even his father's manner of speech, marked by rotund phrases and grandiloquence. Micawber's first speech to David is a caricature of the older Dickens' manner of address. He says: "Under the impression that your peregrinations in this metropolis have not yet been extensive, and that you might have some difficulty in penetrating the arcana of the Modern Babylon in direction of the City Road—in short, that you might lose yourself—I shall be happy to call this evening, and install you in the knowledge of the nearest way." Forster, in his biography of Dickens, contrasted this with some utterances of the actual John Dickens. "I must express my tendency to believe that his longevity is (to say the least of it) extremely problematical," and, "The Supreme Being must be an entirely different individual from what I have every reason to believe Him to be, if He would care in the least for the society of your relations."

One of Micawber's many memorable sayings is a direct quote from John Dickens. When they are parting after his release from prison, Micawber gives the boy this advice: "Annual income twenty pounds, annual expenditure nineteen nineteen six, result happiness. Annual income twenty pounds, annual expenditure twenty pounds ought and six, result misery. The blossom is blighted, the leaf is withered, the God of days goes down upon the dreary scene—and in short you are ever floored. As I am." The first part of this is identical with advice that Dickens said he received from his own father when he visited him in the Marshalsea.

Another small incident from real life is "Mrs. Micawber's

Boarding Establishment for Young Ladies." A brass plate bearing this legend adorned the Micawbers' door, although David "never found that any young lady had ever been to school there; or that any young lady ever came, or proposed to come; or that the least preparation was ever made to receive any young lady." For a time when he was a boy Dickens' own house had borne a plaque, "Mrs. Dickens's Establishment." Young Charles left, at a great many doors, a great many circulars calling attention to the merits of the establishment. But, he told Forster: "Nobody ever came to school, nor do I recollect that anybody ever proposed to come, or that the least preparation was made to receive anybody."

When Mr. Micawber is released from Fleet Street prison he takes his family to Plymouth where relatives of Mrs. Micawber's might obtain for him a place in the customs—he is sure, as always, that "something will turn up." Young David, left alone in London, decides to run away to his father's aunt in Dover, Betsey Trotwood. He has never seen this sardonic female and is not encouraged by memories of the tales his mother had told him of her only visit to the family at the time of his birth. But she is his only relative, so, with a half-guinea borrowed by mail from Peggotty, he sets off on foot to find her. He is promptly robbed of the coin and everything he owns, except the clothing he is wearing and three half-pence in his pocket, by a boy he hired to take his box on a donkey cart to a place of storage.

Young David trudges sadly in the direction of Dover, picturing himself "being found dead in a day or two, under some hedge." He sells his waistcoat for ninepence to an old-clothes dealer, and later his coat, to buy bread which he munches as he limps down the Dover road. Sleeping in hedge rows and haycocks he reaches his destination at the end of three weary and frightening days. When he presents himself to Miss Betsey in her garden he makes a sorry picture; his shoes are broken "until the very shape and form of shoes had departed from them," his shirt and trousers are stained with grass and soil, his hair is uncombed.

His first reception by his formidable aunt is discouraging. "Go away," she cries. "Go along. No boys here." When David discloses their relationship and bursts into tears, she takes the sobbing boy into the house, where she doses him from several bottles taken out of a cupboard. "I think they must have been taken out at random," said David, "for I am sure I tasted aniseseed water, anchovy sauce, and salad dressing." Miss Betsey writes the Murdstones to come and get the boy, but when they appear they are so offensive she imperiously sends them off and decides to keep the lad, changing his name to Trotwood Copperfield after her side of the family.

David's childhood ends when he is adopted by Aunt Betsey. Many critics hold that the first quarter of *David Copperfield*, which is devoted to the first ten or eleven years of the boy's life, is the best part of the book and, indeed, some of the most effective writing in all of Dickens. Except for a couple of minor incidents and the basing of one other character on a real life prototype, the autobiographical nature of the novel ends here. To this point Dickens has portrayed with unequaled feeling, insight, and realism what modern psychologists would consider a typical example of the reactions of an intelligent, sensitive child to parental rejection. But for the influence of the Micawbers and his desperate decision to seek refuge with his unknown aunt, the ten-year-old David might have become a delinquent.

Approximately the next two quarters of the book deal with David the adolescent—a period of relative happiness in contrast to his earlier years. The first six years of it he spends in a good school, well clothed and with ample spending money. While at school he boards with Aunt Betsey's lawyer, Mr. Wickfield, and upon his introduction to this household he meets two other juvenile characters with whom his life is to be entwined throughout the remainder of the book.

The first of these is Uriah Heep, one of Dickens' greatest villains, whose name has become a synonym for pretended humility and repulsive slyness. Uriah, Mr. Wickfield's clerk, is fifteen years old when David first sees his cadaverous face as he comes out to take the bridle of Aunt Betsey's pony chaise with "a long, lank, skeleton hand." His red hair is "cropped as close as the closest stubble"; he has scarcely any eyebrows and no eyelashes—his eyes are so "unsheltered and unshaded" that David wonders how he goes to sleep. He is high shouldered and bony and crouches in a constant half-bow as he wrings his skeletal dry hands together. Uriah repeatedly insists that he is "a very humble person," not worthy of Master Copperfield's friendship, but he will be everlastingly grateful if Master Copperfield will honor his "umble" abode by taking tea with his "umble" mother. Uriah's father had been of a "umble calling," a sexton, but is now "a partaker of glory." So, with his unctuous, fawning manner, Uriah Heep cloaks a deep and slimy villainy which aimed at the control of Mr. Wickfield and the possession of his beautiful daughter.

Agnes, Mr. Wickfield's daughter, is the other youthful character who enters the book at this point. At David's age she is already filling the role of her dead mother as her father's little housekeeper, with a "little basket-trifle hanging at her side, with keys in it; and she looked as staid and as discreet a housekeeper as the old house could have." Standing above

David on the stairs she reminds him of a stained-glass window in a church; "and I associated something of its tranquil brightness with Agnes Wickfield ever afterwards." So Dickens emphasizes, at first meeting, the angelic quality that is the principal theme of Agnes's character—a quality that seems a little bit too good to be true. Like so many of Dickens' characters, Agnes is a mild caricature, in this case a caricature of female nobility and purity.

David enters with some trepidation the fine academy run by Dr. Strong. He knows nothing of the sports and games that the other boys play and has little of their formal academic training. But he is more disturbed by what he does know than by what he does not. He is fearful that his schoolmates will sense his tawdry background: his familiarity with King's Bench prison and the streets of London; what he considers his shameful experience in the warehouse; the pawnings of the Micawber possessions. Because of his background, he recalled: "I felt distrustful of my slightest look and gesture, shrunk within myself whenever I was approached by one of my new schoolfellows, and hurried off, the minute school was over, afraid of committing myself in my response to any friendly notice or advance."

But David soon overcomes his uneasiness in his new surroundings and Dickens describes the six years that he spent in the pleasant atmosphere of the school—where he finally becomes the "head boy"—with what one feels is a somewhat nostalgic "might have been." This is the "good grammar school" that Dickens never had a chance to attend. Because Dickens never had such an experience, there is little that is autobiographical, but several incidents in this section of the novel attest to the writer's keen understanding of the adolescent mind and emotions.

David has not been at school long before Miss Shepherd briefly enters his life. Miss Shepherd is a boarder at the Misses Nettingalls' establishment for girls. David sees her at church and is immediately smitten. In the choristers' chant he hears Miss Shepherd's name, which he mentally inserts in the service—"I put her in among the Royal Family." His bliss is uncontrolled when he meets Miss Shepherd at dancing school. He touches her glove and feels "a thrill go up the right arm of my jacket, and come out at my hair." He proves his love for Miss Shepherd with a gift of twelve Brazil nuts. Why Brazil nuts? He does not know. "They are not expressive of affection; they are difficult to pack into a parcel of any regular shape; they are hard to crack, even in room doors, and they are oily when cracked; yet I feel that they are appropriate for Miss Shepherd." But the affair soon languishes. David hears whispers that Miss Shepherd wishes he would not stare so, and that she has avowed a preference for Master Jones— "for Jones! a boy of no merit whatever!" Then, when he meets Miss Nettingalls' establishment out walking and Miss Shepherd makes a face at him and laughs to her companions as she goes by: "All is over, the devotion of a life—it seems a life, it is all the same—is at an end; Miss Shepherd comes out of the morning service, and the Royal Family knows her no more."

Another brief adolescent interlude has to do with the butcher's boy, who rises "like the apparition of an armed head in *Macbeth*. . . . the terror of the youth of Canterbury." The burly butcher's boy, it is rumored, gets his strength from the beef suet with which he anoints his hair, and is a match for a man. His public castigation of the young gentlemen at Dr. Strong's school and his bullying of the smaller boys is unendurable and David resolves to fight him. The combat,

supervised on David's part by some of his schoolmates and on
the butcher's boy's by "two other butchers, a young publi-
can, and a sweep," is disasterous for David. He is taken home
in a sorry condition to have beefsteaks put on his eyes and his
bruises rubbed with vinegar and brandy. His three days of
recovery are made bearable by Agnes who, he says, "is a sister
to me. . . . I tell her all about the butcher, and the wrongs
that he has heaped upon me; she thinks that I could not have
done otherwise than fight the butcher, while she shrinks and
trembles at my having fought him." This is the beginning of
David's consideration for Agnes as a sister, a misconception of
their emotional relationship that it takes years to rectify.

The teen years pass. As the "head boy" at age seventeen
David can scarcely remember the little fellow who first came
to the school. That creature "seems to be no part of me; I remember him as something left behind upon the road of life—
as something that I have passed, rather than have actually
been." Agnes, too, has changed. The little girl of the first day
at Mr. Wickfield's is now "my sweet sister, my counsellor
and friend, the better angel . . . of all who come within her
calm, good, self-denying influence." David now wears a gold
watch and chain, a ring upon his finger, a long-tailed coat,
"and I use a great deal of bear's grease." In this callow condition he falls in love with the eldest Miss Larkins.

"The eldest Miss Larkins is not a little girl. She is a tall,
dark, black-eyed, fine figure of a woman. The eldest Miss
Larkins is not a chicken; for the youngest Miss Larkins is not
that, and the eldest must be three or four years older. Perhaps
the eldest Miss Larkins may be about thirty. My passion for
her is beyond all bounds."

It is a heart-breaking passion. The eldest Miss Larkins is
acquainted with officers, and the raging agonies that David

suffers on the night of the Race Ball, when he knows that his
enamorata is dancing with the military, "ought to have some
compensations, if there is even-handed justice in the world."
David continually wears his newest silk neckerchief and has
his boots cleaned over and over again to be worthier of the
eldest Miss Larkins. He walks outside the Larkins' home in
the evening, cut to the heart to see the officers go in and
"wishing that a fire would burst out; that the assembled
crowd would stand appalled; that I, dashing through them
with a ladder, might rear it against her window, save her in
my arms, go back for something she has left behind, and
perish in the flames. For I am generally disinterested in my
love, and think that I could be content to make a figure before Miss Larkins and expire."

But there are some brighter visions. When invited to a ball
at the Larkins' home David imagines himself making a declaration to Miss Larkins. "I picture Miss Larkins sinking her
head on my shoulder, and saying, 'Oh, Mr. Copperfield, can
I believe my ears!' I picture Mr. Larkins waiting on me next
morning and saying, 'My dear Copperfield, my daughter has
told me all. Youth is no objection. Here are twenty thousand
pounds. Be happy!'" David goes to the ball, his first
grown-up party. He brashly takes Miss Larkins away from a
Captain Bailey for an enchanted waltz, boldly demands a
flower from her bosom, and is finally introduced to Mr. Chestle, a hop-grower: "a plain elderly gentleman, who has been
playing whist all night." He remains in seventh heaven for
several days after, treasuring the flower, until his aunt tells
him that the eldest Miss Larkins is to be married shortly—not
to the dashing Captain Bailey but to the elderly hop-grower,
Mr. Chestle. Recalls David: "I am terribly dejected for about
a week or two. I take off my ring, I wear my worst clothes,

I use no bear's grease, and I frequently lament over the late Miss Larkins's faded flower. Being, by that time, rather tired of this kind of life, and having received new provocation from the butcher, I throw the flower away, go out with the butcher, and gloriously defeat him. This, and the resumption of my ring, as well as the bear's grease in moderation, are the last marks that I can discern, now, in my progress to seventeen."

Upon David's graduation from school Aunt Betsey treats him to a vacation in London, and here, after the theater, he runs into Steerforth, now an Oxford man in his early twenties. He goes to Steerforth's home, meets his mother, a doting, indulgent parent for whom the sun rises and sets in her handsome, charming, worthless son, who, she avers, is always "generous and noble." There is also the mother's companion, Rosa Dartle, embittered by a hopeless love for young Steerforth even though he, as a child, marked her for life with a scar upon her mouth—an incident that Steerforth casually explained to David by saying: "I was a young boy, and she exasperated me, and I threw a hammer at her. A promising young angel I must have been!"

A third member of the Steerforth menage is the lad's "gentleman's gentleman," Littimer, an unimpeachably respectable character who rouses in David a feeling of fear and awe. David is inordinately conscious of his youth and inexperience in the valet's presence. When Littimer attends him in the morning David feels that "however far I might have been lifted out of myself overnight, and advanced toward maturer years by Steerforth's companionship . . . in the presence of this most respectable man I became, as our smaller poets sing, 'a boy again.'" Littimer brings up the horses that the youths ride, hands the foils and the gloves with which Steerforth introduces David to fencing and boxing. It does not bother David that Steerforth should find him a novice in these skills; "But I never could bear to show my want of skill before the respectable Littimer. I have no reason to believe that Littimer understood such arts himself—he never led me to suppose anything of the kind, by so much as the vibration of one of his respectable eyelashes—yet whenever he was by, while we were practising, I felt myself the greenest and most inexperienced of mortals."

In analyzing Dickens' handling of youthful characters, G.K. Chesterton selected David's attitude toward Littimer as one of the most realistic expositions of the adolescent personality. David finds the manservant more alarming than the lowering Mr. Murdstone, the supercilious Mrs. Steerforth, the unctuous Uriah Heep. Said Chesterton: "A youth of common courage does not fear anything violent, but he is in mortal fear of anything correct." David is afraid that in his inexperience he will do something gauche in the eyes of the ultraconventional Littimer—at this stage of development murder might sometimes be justified, but there could never be justification for spilling the soup.

David plans to conclude his vacation by visiting the Peggottys in Yarmouth and Steerforth agrees to go with him. The older boy had met Dan Peggotty and Ham when they visited David at Salem House. When Rosa Dartle asks Steerforth what kind of people they were, Dickens lays another stone in the foundation of the youth's shallow character by having him reply: "Why, there's a pretty wide separation between them and us," said Steerforth, with indifference. "They are not to be expected to be as sensitive as we are. Their delicacy is not to be shocked, or hurt very easily. They are wonderfully virtuous, I dare say. Some people contend

for that, at least; and I am sure that I don't want to contra-
dict them. But they have not very fine natures, and they may
be thankful that, like their coarse rough skins, they are not
easily wounded." David believes that "Steerforth had said
what he had, in jest, or to draw Miss Dartle out; and I expected him to say as much when she was gone and we two
were sitting before the fire." Steerforth makes no such ad-
mission—he was not jesting—but David still sees his friend
through the golden haze of hero worship that had started in
school.

Steerforth himself bitterly knows his own nature. "It would
be better to be this poor Peggotty," he says moodily, "or his
lout of a nephew, than to be myself, twenty times richer and
twenty times wiser, and to be the torment to myself that I
have been. . . . I wish with all my soul that I had been better
guided! I wish with all my soul I could guide myself better!
. . . David, I wish to God I had had a judicious father in these
last twenty years." And with prophetic vision he tells David:
"If anything should ever separate us, you must think of me at
my best, old boy. Come! Let us make that bargain. Think of
me at my best if circumstances should ever part us."

David and Steerforth arrived at the Peggotty barge home
at an auspicious—or perhaps an inauspicious—time. Little
Em'ly had consented to marry the simple, dependable Ham,
who had silently loved her since boyhood. ". . . a honest sort
of a chap," said Mr. Peggotty, "with his 'art in the right
place." The Oxford man was at his charming best at the Peggottys', showing none of the condescension that he felt toward
these simple people. He told stories of the sea, induced Mr.
Peggotty to sing. Em'ly listened, "and her face got animated."
When they left, Steerforth allowed that Em'ly was "a most
engaging little beauty. . . . Well, it's a quaint place, and they

are quaint company; and it's quite a new sensation to mix with them." Before their final departure Steerforth buys a pleasure boat, renames it the "Little Em'ly," and commissions Dan Peggotty to refurbish it for him. He would have further occasion to visit Yarmouth.

So begins a story within a story that has little to do with the later life of David but recurs intermittently throughout the remainder of the book. The further tale of Little Em'ly, Ham, Steerforth, and Mr. Peggotty is pure, unrealistic melodrama. It could readily be moved from the book to the stage and take its place beside *East Lynn*, the *Old Homestead* and other overdrawn dramas of that era. It must be admitted that Little Em'ly, whose life is irrevocably and permanently ruined by a single act of moral turpitude, is perhaps the least believable youthful character in *David Copperfield*. The depth of the melodrama is indicated by excerpts from the letter she leaves for Ham when she runs away with Steerforth just before the time for her marriage:

"When you, who love me so much better than I have ever deserved, even when my mind was innocent, see this, I shall be far away, and it will be never to come back unless he brings me back a lady . . . Oh, if you knew how my heart is torn. If even you, that I have wronged so much, that never can forgive me, could only know what I suffer. . . . God bless all! I'll pray for all, often, on my knees, If he don't bring me back a lady, and I don't pray for my own self, I'll pray for all. My parting love to uncle. My last tears, and my last thanks, to uncle!"

Equally melodramatic is Mr. Peggotty's speech when he announces that his life henceforth shall be devoted to seeking the fallen child. "Every night, as reg'lar as the night comes, the candle must be stood in its old pane of glass, that if ever she should see it, it may seem to say, 'Come back, my child, come back!' If ever there's a knock, Ham (partic'ler a soft knock), arter dark, at your aunt's door, doen't you go nigh it. Let it be her—not you—that sees my fallen child."

Dickens never gave any reason for Little Em'ly's fall from grace. Perhaps it was Steerforth's irresistible charm, or the lure of far places as a change from the monotony of her shel-tered life, or that she wanted at least the outward appearance of being a lady—a longing that she had first expressed at the age of eight. David finally learned of her further adventures when he was summoned to Mrs. Steerforth's house by Rosa Dartle to meet Littimer. That worthy told how his master and the girl had traveled to France, Switzerland, Italy, "in fact, almost all parts." For a short time all went well. "The young woman was very improvable, and spoke the languages, and wouldn't have been known for the same country per-son." The affair lasted longer than Littimer had expected, until Steerforth finally became annoyed at the girl's more fre-quent spells of low spirits and deserted her in Naples. "But," said the valet, "Mr. James, I must say, certainly did behave extremely honourable; for he proposed that the young woman should marry a very respectable person, who was fully pre-pared to overlook the past, and who was, at least, as good as anybody the young woman could have aspired to in a regular way, her connexions being very common." The "very re-spectable person" was, of course, Littimer.

Peggotty and his niece are finally united in London, with an assist from David, and sail for Australia to start a new life. Years later Old Daniel returns, briefly, to tell David that they had prospered in a mild way. Em'ly never married. She is, said her uncle: "Cheerful along with me; retired when others is by; fond of going any distance fur to teach a child, or fur to tend a sick person, or fur to do some kindness tow'rds a young girl's wedding; . . . fondly loving of her uncle; patient; liked by young and old; sowt out by all that has any trouble. That's Em'ly!"

And what of Steerforth and the spurned suitor Ham? They expire together in a chapter contrived solely for that purpose and titled "The Tempest." David was again in Yarmouth when a tremendous storm swept in from the sea. A boat was in trouble off shore. One by one its occupants were swept over the side until but one remained, clinging to the mast; from which vantage he jauntily waved his red cap. "I saw him do it," said David, "and thought I was going distracted, when his action brought an old remembrance to my mind of a once dear friend."

With a rope around his waist Ham tries to reach the ship, to be dashed to his death against its side as the vessel breaks up. While David sorrowfully surveys his corpse a fisherman directs him to another body that has been washed onto the beach. "He led me to the shore. And on that part of it where she and I had looked for shells, two children—on that part of it where some lighter fragments of the old boat, blown down last night, had been scattered by the wind—among the ruins of the home he had wronged—I saw him lying with his head upon his arm, as I had often seen him lie at school." David bursts into a sorrowing valedictory; "Never more, Oh, God forgive you, Steerforth! to touch that passive hand in love and friendship. Never, never more!"

All of this happened many years after David had first introduced Steerforth into the Peggotty household. In the meanwhile David has been apprenticed to Spenlow and Jorkins to become a proctor in Doctors' Commons—a sort of attorney dealing with probates, divorces, licenses, etc. His aunt pays £1,000 for his apprenticeship and sets him up in small chambers where, at the age of eighteen, he is very much the gentleman. "It was a wonderfully fine thing to walk about town with the key to my house in my pocket, and to know that I could ask any fellow to come home. . . . It was a wonderfully fine thing to let myself in and out, and to come and go without a word to anyone, and to ring Mrs. Crupp up, gasping, from the depths of the earth, when I wanted her—and when she was disposed to come." But at night it is lonely. He misses Agnes to talk to. "After two days and nights, I felt that I had lived there for a year, and yet I was not an hour older, but was quite as much tormented by my own youthfulness as ever."

The most memorable incident of David's bachelor quarters is his first dissipation. Steerforth is involved, with two friends whom he brings to dinner. David is in a fever of excitement that this, his first effort to entertain his friend, should be a success. He lays in a feast from the pastry cook's together with numerous—very numerous—bottles of wine. Steerforth, of course, must preside—in his presence David would not think of taking the head of the table.

By the time the cheese comes round, many toasts have been drunk and David is feeling "singularly cheerful and light-hearted." He holds forth at length on many subjects—whether he knows anything about them is of little consequence. He laughs heartily at his own jokes, insists that he will give a dinner party like this once a week for his fine friends, and with maudlin sincerity assures Steerforth, "You'retheguiding-starofmyexistence." When he catches sight of himself in the mirror, he sees that he looks pale, his eyes have a vacant appearance and "my hair—only my hair, nothing else—looked drunk." At this point he decides that present company should dine with him the next day, and the day after—every day at five o'clock so that they might continually enjoy the pleasure of such fine company.

By the time that somebody suggests that they go to the theater, David's three companions are all sitting in a mist, a long way off. When they start to leave, David finds that "owing to some confusion in the dark, the door was gone." Steerforth laughingly guides him to the stairs and he starts down. "Near the bottom, somebody fell, and rolled down. Somebody else said it was Copperfield. I was angry at that false report, until, finding myself on my back in the passage, I began to feel there might be some foundation in it."

At the theater there are some people on the stage talking about something or other, "but not in the least intelligibly. . . . The whole building looked to me as though it were learning to swim; it conducted itself in such an unaccountable manner, when I tried to steady it." Somebody suggests that they go down to the dress-boxes where the ladies are and David suddenly finds himself in a box with Agnes, whom he greets with joyful effusion, unmindful of the shushing and cries for "silence" from neighboring boxes. Agnes finally prevails upon him to go home, and the last he remembers is Steerforth undressing him while he takes turns telling him that Agnes is his sister and adjuring him to bring the corkscrew to open another bottle of wine.

Next morning he feels as though "my outer covering of skin was hard as a board; my tongue the bottom of an empty kettle, furred with long service, and burning up over a slow fire; the palms of my hands, hot plates of metal which no ice could cool!" But his agony of mind was worse: the remorse, the shame at having committed a thousand offenses that he had forgotten, and at the thought of the sad and reproachful look that Agnes had bestowed upon him: ". . . my disgust of the very sight of the room where the revel had been held—my racking head—the smell of smoke, the sight of glasses, the impossibility of going out, or even getting up! Oh, what a day it was!"

At about this point Tommy Traddles reenters the story; a youth of about twenty who is still chubby and merry as he reads law in the face of poverty and adversity. David visits him in his little room on a street where "the inhabitants appeared to have a propensity to throw any little trifles they were not in want of, into the road." Somehow the street and house remind him of his days with the Micawbers. Traddles is engaged to a "dear girl," a curate's daughter, one of ten sisters down in Devonshire. He is not fazed by the fact that it will be a long engagement—"wait and hope" is their motto. With supreme optimism he has purchased two pieces of furniture for their some-day home: a flowerpot stand and a little round marble-topped table, which he keeps under a white cloth in the corner of his room. All in all, he tells David: "I get on as well as I can. I don't make much, but I don't spend much. In general, I board with the people downstairs, who are very agreeable people indeed. Both Mr. and Mrs. Micawber have seen a good deal of life, and are excellent company."

So David is reunited with the Micawbers, who have not changed. Mr. Micawber, at the moment, is facing some financial difficulties, but is sure that "something will turn up." David warns Tommy not to lend him money, and Tommy assures him that there is no danger of this—he does not have any. But he does sign a note for Micawber, which leads to the sheriff seizing his two pieces of furniture.

When David visits the Wickfields at this time he finds that great changes have taken place. Mr. Wickfield has been drinking steadily, and Uriah Heep, now in his early twenties, has forced himself into a partnership with the older man, who seems to live in fear of him. Uriah assures David that he is merely the 'umble instrument 'umbly serving that worthy man, Mr. Wickfield, but adds that he has a confidence that he would impart to none but Master Copperfield. 'Umble as he is, and 'umble as his mother is, "and lowly as our poor but honest roof has ever been, the image of Miss Agnes . . . has been in my breast for years. Oh, Master Copperfield, with what pure affection do I love the ground my Agnes walks on." Further, Uriah intimates that he is so *useful* to her father, and Agnes is so attached to her father, "that I think she may come, on his account, to be kind to me." At the image of Agnes, "outraged by so much as a thought of this red-headed animal," David had the delirious idea of swiping the red-hot poker out of the fire and running him through with it; but the sense of power that was in Uriah's face restrained him.

The final youthful character in *David Copperfield* is the teen-age daughter of one of David's employers, Dora Spenlow. He first saw the lovely Dora—"a Fairy, a Sylph"—when he went to dinner at Mr. Spenlow's home. "All was over in a moment. I loved Dora Spenlow to distraction."

Dora's real life counterpart in Dickens' life was eighteen-year-old Maria Beadwell, whom the writer first saw when, at the age of seventeen, *he* went to dinner at the home of her banker father, and promptly fell in love. Maria was a flighty and flirtatious miss and Dickens a typically lovesick swain until the girl's parents whisked her off to Paris, an event which caused his existence to be "entirely uprooted" and made his "whole being blighted." When Maria returned she called him "a boy." With that "short and dreadful word" scorching his brain, he sought oblivion and found a dreadful headache.

This may have been the basis for his description of David's drunken dissipation.

Dickens' love for Maria petered out by the time he reached his maturity. David does not get off so easily—he marries the girl, but not until he has suffered agonies of young love and the cruel denial of her hand by her father. Of that first meeting, recalls David: "I don't remember who was there, except Dora. I have not the least idea of what we had for dinner, besides Dora. My impression is that I dined off Dora entirely, and sent away half-a-dozen plates untouched. I sat next to her. I talked to her. She had the most delightful little voice, the gayest little laugh, the pleasantest and most fascinating little ways that ever led a lost youth into hopeless slavery. She was rather diminutive altogether. So much the more precious, I thought."

Dora is not flirtatious; she does not trifle with David's affections as her real life counterpart had apparently trifled with Dickens'. Rather, Dora is adorably impractical and child-like in her view of life and marriage—for the two young people soon had an "understanding." When Dora's father learns of this, he denies the boy the house; but this problem is shortly solved by Spenlow's sudden death. David brings his bride-to-be a cookery book and a household account book, but the cookery book made her head ache and the figures made her cry. She would much rather play with her lap dog, Jip, who had a strong aversion to David. When David told her that the going would be hard at first after they were married, she said he was dreadful to talk about such unpleasant things, and when he mentioned "the crust well-earned—," she interrupted to say: "I don't want to hear any more about crusts! And Jip must have a mutton chop every day at twelve, or he'll die."

David found Dora's childlike refusal to face reality charming. True, he told Agnes that she was rather difficult to—he was going to say rely on, but he changed it to say that "she is a timid little thing, and easily disturbed and frightened . . . as easily scared as a bird." He does not see that these qualities detract from her merit as a wife and does not understand Aunt Betsey's comment when he tells her of his plans to marry Dora: "Ah, Trot!" said Aunt Betsey, "Blind, blind, blind." Although without knowing why, he feels "a vague unhappy loss or want of something overshadow me like a cloud." David was just twenty-one when he married Dora.

Meanwhile, Aunt Betsey has lost all her money and comes to live in his bachelor's quarters with him. Released from his apprenticeship by Spenlow's death, he has studied shorthand and makes a reasonable living reporting debates in the House of Commons, as had his creator at the same age. In the only political note in the book, Dickens has David voice his opinion of British government thusly: "Night after night, I record predictions that never come to pass, professions that are never fulfilled, explanations that are only meant to mystify. I wallow in words. Britannia, that unfortunate female, is always before me, like a trussed fowl, skewered through and through with office pens, and bound hand and foot with red tape. I am sufficiently behind the scenes to know the worth of political life. I am quite an infidel about it and shall never be converted." David augmented his income, as had his creator, by writing pieces for the magazines and was on his way to becoming a successful author.

Critics have noted that *David Copperfield* becomes a somewhat different book after the protagonist reaches his majority. The first quarter of the book is a description of the world as seen through the eyes of a child—or, rather, of a man's memories of the world that he knew in his childhood. The center section is an account of adolescent development and of what happened to that adolescent. The final section is less of a biography. In it David more or less stands off and becomes a storyteller. The important incidents are things that happen to those around him, rather than to David. It is more of a story of the Wickfields and Uriah Heep, of the Micawbers, of Peggoty and Little Em'ly and Steerforth, of Aunt Betsey, than a story of David. It is as though the character of David became static and less interesting to his creator after he passed his youth.

An exception to this is the description of David's brief marriage to Dora, who is still in her late teens, physically, but emotionally retarded. Physically she is attractive and adorable. Intellectually and emotionally she is a playmate, rather than a companion, for her husband. She sings sweetly to the guitar and makes delightful flower paintings, but of housekeeping, food procurement and preparation, the supervision of the maidservants, of which they had a procession, each less capable than the preceding one, she knows nothing and cannot learn. When David seeks to remonstrate with her she pleads: "Don't be a naughty Blue Beard! Don't be serious!" She cries because she thinks he is going to scold her and when he explains that he is only trying to reason with her, she replies: "But reasoning is worse than scolding! I didn't marry to be reasoned with." At such times David suffers "such pangs of remorse as made me miserable. I had the conscience of an assassin, and was haunted by a vague sense of enormous wickedness."

Dora sums up her conception of marriage by asking David to call her a special name—his "child-wife." She tells him: "When you want to be angry with me, say to yourself, 'It's only my child-wife!' When I am very disappointing, say, 'I knew, a long time ago, that she would make but a child-wife!' When you miss what I should like to be, and I think can never be, say, 'Still my child-wife loves me!' For indeed I do."

David soon realizes that he cannot mold Dora's mind or character. Both are already developed as far as they will go, leaving her, emotionally and intellectually, a perennial child. He realizes that he is missing something, a counselor, a companion, but becomes resigned that this cannot be. "Thus it was that I took upon myself the toils and cares of our life, and had no partner in them." Finally, David concluded: "I had endeavored to adapt Dora to myself, and found it impracticable. It remained for me to adapt myself to Dora; to share with her what I could, and be happy; to bear on my own shoulders what I must, and still be happy. This was the discipline to which I tried to bring my heart, when I began to think. It made my second year much happier than the first; and, what was better still, made Dora's life all sunshine."

The second year of the marriage is the last. Before it ends, Dora sickens and dies. Her last moments are spent privately, at her request, with Agnes. David learns, much later, that she has made Agnes promise to take her place. Even her childish intellect realized, perhaps intuitively, that this was something that Agnes has always wanted, and that David, unconsciously, has the same feeling.

Thus ends the story of the youthful characters in *David Copperfield*. Everyone is now grown up and all get their just deserts. Mr. Micawber, working as Uriah Heep's clerk, unmasks his villainy with the aid of Traddles, now a successful lawyer. Uriah is forced to make restitution, including Aunt Betsey's money, which he had feloniously acquired. The Micawbers go to Australia on the boat with Peggotty and Little

Em'ly and, some time later, a newspaper comes back with an account of a testimonial dinner given to Wilkens Micawber, the successful and respected magistrate. Traddles marries his "dear girl" and is well on his way to a judgeship, while he lives merrily in a large house with a bevy of sisters-in-law. He hears that Mr. Creakle has become a Middlesex magistrate, in charge of a jail, and he and David visit the old schoolmaster. Here they meet two prisoners in adjoining cells. One is Uriah Heep, a model prisoner who is still "very 'umble." The other is Littimer, from whom they learn that Mr. Murdstone has married another unfortunate young woman, "with a very good little property." And, of course, David marries Agnes.

Through the years there have been countless critiques on *David Copperfield*. Many laud it nauseously, a few condemn it viciously; as with much that has been written about Dickens, there is little objectivity. Perhaps G.K. Chesterton expressed the merit of *David Copperfield* best by writing: "When we say the book is true to life we must stipulate that it is especially true to youth; even to boyhood. All the characters seem a little larger than they really were, for David is looking up at them. . . . We have Murdstone as he would be to a boy who hated him; and rightly, for a boy would hate him. We have Steerforth as he would be to a boy who adored him; and rightly, for a boy would adore him." More than any other book of Dickens', *David Copperfield* is concerned in the common actualities in the life of a boy from infancy through adolescence, actualities that are treated with romantic realism. As Chesterton says: "This life of heroes and villains is life as it is lived. The life a man knows best is exactly the life he finds most full of fierce certainties and battles between good and ill—his own."

CHAPTER

III

CHILDREN OF GOOD AND EVIL

"But for the mercy of God, I might easily have been . . . a little robber or a little vagabond," said ten-year-old David Copperfield. But for David, who always had some adult guidance on the path of rectitude, such a course was never more than a remote possibility. Not so fortunate was Oliver Twist, who at a like age was completely alone, surrounded by callous or thoroughly disreputable adults: ". . . a poor, houseless, wandering boy, without a friend to help him, or a roof to shelter his head." His story is the triumph of innate goodness over the forces of evil: ". . . a sulphurous melodrama in which horror is fused with angry pathos."

Oliver Twist, written some twelve years before *David Copperfield*, was Dickens' first planned novel and the first novel in the English language with a child as its center of focus. (*Pickwick Papers*, the only lengthy piece of writing that preceded it, had been conceived as a series of magazine stories and had grown into a full-length book more or less by chance.) *Oliver Twist* is also Dickens' principal "message novel," the one which contributes most to his reputation as a social crusader or reformer. His purpose behind the lurid, melodramatic fictional tale was to expose to his readers the horrors of the workhouses into which the poor were forced, the callous imhumanity of the authorities who ran them, the iniquities of the baby farms that were adjuncts to such institutions, and the seething sea of dirt and disease and crime and vice to which the social conditions of the day condemned the great mass of the city poor. All of this he presents, sometimes with cruel humor, as the background against which young Oliver interacts with the boy thieves Charley Bates and the Artful Dodger; the bullying charity boy, Noah Claypole; the teen-age trollop Nancy; as well as the adult villains Fagan, Sikes, and Monks.

For years after it was published Dickens felt called upon to defend this excursion into the seamy side of life; this presentation of thieves and criminals in terms of filth and utter degradation rather than through the romanticism and excitement of the velvet-coated, jack-booted highwayman, a common fictional figure of the day. In the preface to the third edition he wrote: "What manner of life is that which is described in these pages, as the everyday existence of a Thief? What charms has it for the young and ill-disposed, what allurements for the most jolterheaded of juveniles? Here are no canterings upon moonlit heaths, no merrymakings in the snuggest of all possible caverns, none of the attractions of dress, no embroidery, no lace, no jack boots, no crimson coats, none of the dash and freedom with which 'the road' has been, time out of mind, invested. The cold, wet, shelterless midnight streets of London; the foul and drowsy dens where vice is closely packed and lacks the room to turn; the haunts

of hunger and disease; the shabby rags that scarcely hold together; where are the attractions of these things? Have they
no lesson, and do they not whisper something beyond the
little-regarded warning of a moral precept?" Dickens had
little patience with those who were too refined and delicate
to "contemplate such horrors": readers for whom reality
"must be, like their meat, in delicate disguise." For among
such, he said: "It is wonderful how Virtue turns from dirty
stockings; and how Vice, married to ribbons and a little gay
attire, changes her name, as wedded ladies do, and becomes
Romance." He would not, "for these readers, abate one hole
in the Dodger's coat, or one scrap of curlpaper in the girl's
dishevelled hair."

Dickens insisted that the background against which he
presented Oliver was one of stark realism, and historians
agree, though some make the point that the social conditions
which Dickens portrayed were in the course of correction before he wrote—that the picture that he paints is more typical
of the late years of the eighteenth century and the early years
of the nineteenth than of the 1830s. But in one aspect the
book, by the standards of many twentieth-century authors,
is unrealistic. Most modern writers, reporting on characters
such as these, would consider it necessary—or lifelike—to re-
produce the vulgarity and obscenity of their speech and portray their sexual immorality. Dickens agreed with many
readers—then and now—that such realism may be unneces-
sarily offensive. Seventeen-year-old Nancy lives openly with
the adult thief, Bill Sikes, but no point is made of the physical aspect of their relationship. The discourse of Charley Bates
and the Artful Dodger, who have known no homes except
the streets of London's slums, is earthy but never obscene.

Oliver himself, whose only school and home was the work-house, talks like a little gentleman.

In opening the story of Oliver Twist, Dickens loses little time in couching his lance against the callous disregard for the children of the poor that was represented by the workhouse system. Oliver is born on the first page and almost dies on the second, despite (or perhaps because of, says Dickens with sardonic humor) the very casual attentions of a parish sur-geon, "who did such matters by contract," and a pauper old woman, "who was rendered rather misty by an unwonted allowance of beer," and who was qualified for her obstetrical office only by the fact that she had had thirteen children of her own; " . . . and all of them dead except two, and them in the wurkus with me." Oliver's mother, who had crept into the workhouse the night before, wearing no wedding ring, quietly expired as her new-born son emitted his first cry.

Since there was no female domiciled in the workhouse who was in a condition to render Oliver the consolation and nourishment of which he stood in need, the parochial au-thorities placed him at a baby farm "where twenty or thirty other juvenile offenders against the poor-laws rolled about the floor all day, without the inconvenience of too much food or too much clothing, under the parental supervision of an el-derly female, who received the culprits at and for the con-sideration of sevenpence-halfpenny per small head per week." This crone held that too much to eat was not good for very young children, so she appropriated the greater part of the weekly stipend for her own use. The little paupers were most unappreciative. "At the very moment when a child had con-trived to exist upon the smallest possible portion of the weak-est food, it did perversely happen, in eight and a half cases out of ten, either that it sickened from want and cold, or fell into the fire from neglect, or got half-smothered by accident; in any one of which cases, the miserable little being was usually summoned into another world, and there gathered to the fathers it had never known in this."

Oliver was one of the 15 per cent who survived the sparse diet and rigorous treatment, and is next met on his ninth birthday, which he is celebrating in a coal cellar, together with two other young gentlemen who have been confined there after a sound thrashing, for "atrociously presuming to be hungry." Oliver was now "a pale, thin child, somewhat diminutive in stature, and decidedly small in circumference," but with a sturdy spirit that nature or inheritance had implanted in his breast, where it had plenty of room to expand, "thanks to the spare diet of the establishment." It was on this day that Mr. Bumble, the beadle, made a surprise visit for the purpose of taking Oliver back to the main workhouse. Mrs. Mann, the baby-farm manager, had to distract him with a drop of gin—which she kept only "to put into the blessed infants when they ain't well"—until an older girl could spirit Oliver and his companions upstairs and make them presentable.

At the workhouse Oliver is interviewed by the board—a group of "philosophers," said Dickens, who believed that the poor liked the workhouse, considered it "a regular place of public entertainment . . . a tavern where there was nothing to pay." So the board, in their wisdom, "established the rule that all the poor people should have the alternative (for they would compel nobody, not they) of being starved by a gradual process in the house, or by a quick one out of it." One of these wise gentlemen, with a gruff voice, advises Oliver that he had come there to be educated and taught a useful trade; "So you'll begin to pick oakum tomorrow morning at

six o'clock." The boy is then provided with a blanket and a
board bed in a large room and allowed to sob himself to sleep.
"What a noble illustration of the tender laws of England"
wrote Dickens. "They let the paupers go to sleep!"

Dickens' description of Oliver's diet in the workhouse—
"three meals of thin gruel a day, with an onion twice a week,
and half a roll on Sundays"—was an exaggeration, but not a
gross one. Children in the workhouse were to be fed "at discretion," and in many cases the discretion of economy-
minded managers provided a diet that was not sufficient for
subsistence. In any event, Dickens' description of Oliver's asking for more is the most memorable passage in the novel,
worthy of quoting at length.

"The room in which the boys were fed," wrote Dickens,
"was a large stone hall, with a copper at one end, out of which
the master, dressed in an apron for the purpose, and assisted
by one or two women, ladled the gruel at mealtimes. Of this
festive composition each boy had one porringer, and no more
—except on occasions of great public rejoicing, when he had
two ounces and a quarter of bread besides. The bowls never
wanted washing. The boys polished them with their spoons
till they shown again; and when they had performed this
operation (which never took very long; the spoons were
nearly as large as the bowls), they would sit staring at the
copper, with such eager eyes, as if they could have devoured
the very bricks of which it was composed; employing themselves, meanwhile, in sucking their fingers assiduously, with
the view of catching up any stray splashes of gruel that might
have been cast thereon. Boys have generally excellent appe-
tites. Oliver Twist and his companions suffered the tortures
of slow starvation for three months. At last they got so
voracious and wild with hunger that one boy, who was tall

for his age, and hadn't been used to that sort of thing (for his father had kept a small cook-shop), hinted darkly to his companions that unless he had another basin of gruel *per diem*, he was afraid that he might some night happen to eat the boy who slept next to him, who happened to be a weakly youth of tender age. He had a wild, hungry eye; and they implicitly believed him. A council was held; lots were cast who should walk up to the master after supper that evening, and ask for more; and it fell to Oliver Twist.

"The evening arrived; the boys took their places. The master, in his cook's uniform, stationed himself at the copper; his pauper assistants ranged themselves behind him; the gruel was served out; and a long grace was said over the short commons. The gruel disappeared; the boys whispered to each other, and winked at Oliver; while his next neighbors nudged him. Child as he was, he was desperate with hunger, and reckless with misery. He rose from the table; and advancing to the master, basin and spoon in hand, said, somewhat alarmed at his own temerity:

" 'Please, sir, I want some more.'

"The master was a fat, healthy man; but he turned very pale. He gazed in stupefied astonishment on the small rebel for some seconds, then clung for support to the copper. The assistants were paralyzed with wonder; the boys with fear.

" 'What!' said the master at length, in a faint voice.

" 'Please, sir,' replied Oliver, 'I want some more.'

"The master aimed a blow at Oliver's head with the ladle, pinioned him in his arms, and shrieked aloud for the beadle."

The board was sitting in high and solemn conclave when Mr. Bumble rushed in excitedly to tell them that Oliver Twist had asked for more. After they had recovered from their astonishment at an ungrateful pauper lad who would ask for more after he had consumed the supper allotted by the dietary, one board member gasped, "That boy will be hung. I know that boy will be hung." But in a calmer mood they finally decide that Oliver should be immediately placed in solitary confinement and that a sign should be promptly pasted on the outside gate offering five pounds to anybody who would take Oliver Twist off the hands of the parish.

Apprenticing parish orphans was another aspect of the poor laws against which Dickens crusaded vigorously. The parish authorities were permitted to offer a fee of five pounds, plus a suit of clothes for the victim, to any master who would take a child off their hands—often one of tender years—and keep him until he reached his majority. Such masters were supposed to teach the youngsters a trade, but so long as the parish got rid of the child there was usually little interest in what the master did with him. At best many boys became pot boys or hostler's helpers, girls household drudges. At worst the boys ended as pickpockets and thieves, the girls as prostitutes.

Among the least desirable masters for parish orphan boys were chimney sweeps, who, because small stature was a necessity in the work, frequently took boys as young as six. To point up the horror of using youngsters for this work, Dickens has a chimney sweep propose to take Oliver. When one of the members of the board offers a mild objection that young boys had been smothered in chimneys, the sweep replies: "That's 'cause they damped the straw afore they lit it in the chimbley to make 'em come down agin. That's all smoke and no blaze; vereas smoke ain't o' no use at all in makin' a boy come down, for it only sinds him to sleep, and that's wot he likes. Boys is wery obstinit, and wery lazy, gen-'l'men, and there's nothink like a good hot blaze to make 'em come down with a run. It's humane, too, gen'l'men, acause, even if they've stuck in the chimbley, roasting their feet makes 'em struggle to hextricate themselves." The logic of this explanation overcomes the scruples of the board member; but Oliver is saved from this fate by a magistrate who refuses to approve the indentures.

The next applicant for Oliver's services is Mr. Sowerberry, the undertaker, who makes a good thing of disposing of the workhouse dead. He complains at the low fees that the parish allows, but Mr. Bumble points out, quite rightly, that paupers never require commodious coffins, and there is a considerable saving in materials in providing boxes for such emaciated corpses. However, it is agreed that Mr. Sowerberry's services to the parish entitle him to some consideration, and the obligation is met by giving him Oliver and the five pounds. The youngster is led off to the undertaking establishment by Mr. Bumble and even that hardened parochial officer is moved by Oliver's piteous cry at being forced out into an unknown and frightening world: "I am a very little boy, sir, and it is so lonely, sir. Everybody hates me. Oh! sir, don't, don't pray be cross with me."

Oliver's reception at the undertakers is not reassuring. Mrs. Sowerberry, "a short, thin, squeezed-up woman with a vixenish countenance," after complaining of his small stature, pushes him down a steep flight of stairs into a stone cell that was called a kitchen and tells a slatternly young servant girl, Charlotte, to give him some of the cold bits that were put by for the dog. "I dare say the boy isn't too dainty to eat 'em—are you, boy?" Oliver, his eyes glistening at the mention of meat, avidly devours the plate of coarse food. At which point Dickens digresses to castigate again the ruling class that supported such heartless and callous treatment of the children of the poor.

"I wish some well-fed philosopher," wrote Dickens (who used the word philosopher to denote a political economist), "whose meat and drink turn to gall within him, whose blood is ice, whose heart is iron, could have seen Oliver Twist clutching at the dainty viands that the dog had neglected. I wish he could have witnessed the horrible avidity with which Oliver tore the bits asunder with all the ferocity of famine. There is only one thing I should like better; and that would be to see the philosopher making the same sort of meal himself, with the same relish."

After completing his dainty meal Oliver is shown his bed, under the counter in the showroom among the coffins, a frightening place dominated by an unfinished coffin with black tassels, "from which he almost expected to see some frightful form slowly rear its head, to drive him mad with terror." Huddled in a little recess beneath the counter, entirely alone in the world, he almost wishes that his narrow bed was the coffin it resembled, in which he could repose in calm and lasting sleep in the churchyard.

Next morning Oliver is awakened by another boy who works for the undertaker, Noah Claypole. Noah is a loutish charity-school boy, not an orphan. "His genealogy went all the way back to his parents, his mother being a washerwoman and his father a drunken soldier." Although big and lumbering, he is, like all bullys, at heart a coward and has never dared take exception to the taunts of neighboring shopboys who deride him with the epithet "charity." Now that a nameless orphan is thrown at his mercy—and a small one, at that—he immediately makes it clear that he proposes to vent his venom on Oliver by kicking him out to take down the shutters.

Oliver had been at the undertaker's for some three months when Mr. Sowerberry one day realized that his small size, good looks, and melancholy expression could be turned into a business asset. Oliver would make a fine juvenile mute—a professional mourner to serve at childrens' funerals. No other undertaker had such a specialty. After gaining experience by accompanying his master on several gruesome expeditions to lay out and measure corpses and attend at the burials, Oliver is fitted with a high, crepe-dressed hat and a black staff and takes his place in the funeral processions of children. As there was a measles epidemic at the time that was widely fatal to infant existence, "many were the mournful processions which little Oliver headed, in a hat-band reaching to his knees, to the indescribable admiration and emotion of all the mothers in the town."

Oliver's career as a mute brings an increase in his mistreatment by Noah Claypole, who is jealous of the new boy's added stature. The maid Charlotte abuses him because Noah does, and Mrs. Sowerberry treats him unkindly because her husband mildly favors him—after all, Oliver is now a business asset. The boy bears up under this threefold unkindness until an occasion when Noah, trying to make him cry, disparages his dead mother. She was, said Noah, "a regular right-down bad 'un, Work'us," and it was well that she died when she did, else she would now be laboring in Bridewell prison, if she had not been transported or hung. Whereat Oliver goes berserk and knocks the bully down.

This incident marks a turning point in his career. After he is beaten and confined in a dust cellar through the combined efforts of his three tormentors, Noah is sent for Mr. Bumble,

to whom he reports that Oliver had tried to murder him and
Charlotte and "the missus." The cause of Oliver's rebellion
is obvious, the beadle tells Mrs. Sowerberry: "Meat, ma'am,
meat. You've over-fed him, ma'am. You've raised a artificial
soul and spirit in him, ma'am, unbecoming a person in his
condition . . . What have paupers to do with soul and spirit?
It's quite enough that we let them have live bodies. If you had
kept the boy on gruel, ma'am, this would never have happened." So Oliver is again beaten by Mr. Sowerberry, at his
wife's insistence, with a few added cuts from Mr. Bumble's
cane.

At dawn the next day Oliver runs away. He knows not
where he is going until, a few miles out of town, he sees a
sign, "London—70 miles." With his total possessions—a clean
shirt, two pairs of stockings, and a penny—he starts on the
seventy-mile walk, begging on the way. Seven days later, after
many minor mishaps, he reaches a suburb of the metropolis.
Here, as he sits with bleeding feet and covered with dust on a
doorstep, he meets one of Dickens' most engaging young
rogues, John Dawkins, better known as the Artful Dodger.

The Dodger is about Oliver's own age, perhaps eleven or
twelve. He was, thought Oliver, one of the queerest-looking
boys that he had ever seen. "He was a snub-nosed, flat-
browed, common-faced boy enough, and as dirty a juvenile
as one would want to see; but he had about him the airs and
manners of a man. He was short for his age: with rather bow-
legs, and little, sharp, ugly eyes. . . . He wore a man's coat,
which reached nearly to his heels. He had turned the cuffs
back, halfway up his arm, to get his hands out of the sleeves,
apparently with the ultimate view of thrusting them into the
pockets of his corduroy trousers, for there he kept them. He
was, altogether, as roystering and swaggering a young gen-

tleman as ever stood four-feet-six, or something less, in his bluchers."

After hearing Oliver's piteous story, the Dodger offers to take his new acquaintance to London and introduce him to "a 'spectable old genelman as lives there, wot'll give you lodgings for nothing, and never ask for change." The Dodger is reluctant to travel by the light of day, so it is long past sundown before the two boys approach the abode of Oliver's future benefactor. As they near it Dickens describes the neighborhood through which they pass: the first of several views of the fetid London slums that were the background for Oliver's stay among thieves. Almost twenty years after Dickens wrote *Oliver Twist*, when his descriptions of this seamy side of London were quoted in support of what is now called an urban renewal project, several public men insisted that these places that the writer presented with a dreadful and concrete reality were figments of his imagination—which they definitely were not. It was Dickens the reporter, not the novelist, who thus described Oliver's first impression of London:

"A dirtier or more wretched place he had never seen. The street was very narrow and muddy, and the air was impregnated with filthy odours. There were a good many small shops; but the only stock in trade seemed to be heaps of children, who, even at that time of night, were crawling in and out of the doors, or screaming from the inside. The sole places that seemed to prosper amid the general blight of the place were the public-houses; and in them, the lowest order of Irish were wrangling with might and main. Covered ways and yards, which here and there diverged from the main street, disclosed little knots of houses, where drunken men and women were positively wallowing in filth; and from several of the doorways, great ill-looking fellows were cautiously emerging, bound, to all appearances, on no very well-disposed or harmless errands."

Into one of these disreputable buildings the Dodger leads Oliver; up a dark stair and, after giving the password, "plummy and slam," into a room of which the walls and ceiling are perfectly black with age and dirt. Here an old man, dressed in a greasy flannel gown, is huddled over a frying pan in the fireplace, cooking sausages. The "villainous-looking and repulsive face" of this shriveled individual is "obscured by a quantity of matted red hair." This is Fagin, a fence and the leader and trainer of a band of boy pickpockets and thieves, some of whom live in this place which will be Oliver's home. There are several rough beds made of old sacks on the floor, and seated around a deal table are four or five boys of about Oliver's age, "smoking long clay pipes and drinking spirits with the air of middle-aged men."

The only one of these several juveniles whom Dickens identifies, other than the Dodger, is Charley Bates, who is presented as something of a simpleton, laughing uproariously at every happening, regardless of its real humor. Next morning another youthful character makes her appearance; seventeen-year-old Nancy, who has been a thief under Fagin's direction since the age of five and who is now the mistress of an adult associate of the old man's, Bill Sikes. On this occasion Nancy is accompanied by another girl, Bet, both of them, said Dickens, "wore a good deal of hair, not very neatly turned up behind, and were rather untidy about shoes and stockings. They were not exactly pretty, perhaps, but they had a good deal of colour in their faces, and looked quite stout and hearty. Being remarkably free and agreeable in their manners, Oliver thought them very nice girls indeed."

After breakfast, Fagin, Charley Bates, and the Dodger play what Oliver considers a very "curious and uncommon" game. The old man puts a snuff box in one trouser pocket, a note case in the other, a watch in his waistcoat, and a spectacle case and handkerchief in other repositories. He then buttons up his coat and walks slowly around the room, stopping at times to pretend that he is looking in a shop window. The two young thieves follow him, dodging to keep out of his sight, until the Dodger steps on his toe, seemingly by accident. As Fagin turns Charley bumps into him and the two boys quickly relieve him of his possessions. Whenever Fagin felt a hand touch his pocket he cried out, and the game was repeated over and over again, to Oliver's delight and amusement.

Such a school for pickpockets was not a product of Dickens' imagination. The records of Old Bailey describe the testimony of a youth who was trained in such a school to pick pockets and rob shops. An autobiography, *Sixty Years of Waifdom*, published somewhat later in the century, tells of a thief's tutor who bragged that he had taught over five hundred children in some twenty years.

After the other boys have gone out to work, Fagin lets Oliver play a simple version of the game by placing his handkerchief in his pocket with one end hanging out and telling Oliver to try to remove it without being detected. When he succeeds the old rogue gives him a shilling and tells him that his skill marks him as a potential great man. Oliver could not understand how picking a pocket in play advanced his chances of being a great man, but assumed that Fagin must know best. During the ensuing days Oliver works at taking monograms out of handkerchiefs, of which the Dodger and Charley brought a great many home. The lad is impressed with the "stern morality" of old Fagin. "Whenever the Dodger or

Charley Bates came home at night empty-handed, he would expiate with great vehemence on the misery of idle and lazy habits, and would enforce upon them the necessity of an active life, by sending them supperless to bed."

Oliver is completely innocent of the nature of the work that the other boys do, and of the source of the handkerchiefs and jewelry and watches that they bring home to Fagin. He, too, wants to earn his keep and importunes Fagin to let him work with them. When this finally happens and he sees the Dodger pick the pocket of an old man browsing at a bookstall, he is appalled. Confused and frightened, he takes to his heels, whereat the old gentleman, Mr. Brownlow, raises the cry: "Stop thief." After a chase Oliver is caught and brought before a magistrate.

Dickens patterned many of his kindly and humorous characters on real life models, but this magistrate, whom he dubbed Mr. Fang, was one of the few odious characters whom he frankly and deliberately based on a living person. He wrote to a friend who had influence in the courts that he needed a magistrate for *Oliver Twist*, and "casting about for a magistrate whose harshness and insolence would render him a fit subject to be *shown up*, I have as a necessary consequence stumbled upon Mr. Laing of Hatton-Garden celebrity." He asked his friend to smuggle him into the Hatton-Garden court to observe the magistrate at work. The result was a characterization of the fictitious magistrate Mr. Fang as hot-tempered, intolerant, harsh, and somewhat stupid in his relations with Mr. Brownlow and Oliver. It may have been a coincidence that, shortly after *Oliver Twist* appeared, the home secretary removed Mr. Laing from office.

Mr. Fang's handling of Oliver in court is so brutal that the boy faints and does not hear the magistrate, over Mr. Brownlow's protestations, sentence him to three months at hard labor—a situation that is saved by the appearance, in the nick of time, of the proprietor of the bookstall at which Mr. Brownlow had been browsing. The bookstore owner had seen the Dodger pick Mr. Brownlow's pocket and testified to Oliver's innocence. The kindly Brownlow takes the unconscious boy to his home.

This is the beginning of a series of incidents and coincidences in the story line of the novel that many critics aver defy belief. Oliver is successively befriended by two good Samaritans. The first, Mr. Brownlow, turns out to be an old friend of his father's. There is a picture of Oliver's mother in his home that has a remarkable resemblance to the boy. The second, Rose Maylie, turns out to be his aunt—although neither knows this at the time. A sinister figure named Monks turns up, who is Oliver's half brother. Oliver's birth is admittedly illegitimate, but Dickens makes the legitimate son, Monks, a complete scoundrel and the bastard Oliver the symbol of goodness—an indication of Dickens' ready sympathy for the unfortunate and downtrodden. There is an estate involved of which Oliver will inherit his half share only if he reaches his majority with his name unstained by an act "of dishonor, meanness, cowardice, or wrong." To prevent Oliver from getting his share the evil Monks bribes Fagin to seduce him into a life of crime; this is Fagin's reason, although it is not known at the time, for being so anxious to recapture Oliver.

After nursing Oliver back to health, Brownlow and his housekeeper become very fond of him. His rags are replaced by fine raimant when he is sent to return some books to a bookstore, with a five-pound note to pay for others that Mr. Brownlow kept. Meanwhile, Fagin knows only that a fine gentleman took the boy away from the court in a carriage, and he has had the Dodger, Bates, Nancy, and Sikes constantly searching for him. Nancy spots him on the street while he is on his errand, summons Sikes from a nearby tavern, and they take the boy back to Fagin. Oliver appeals in vain for protection from bystanders, but Nancy assures them that he is her young brother who has run away from his parents and "joined a set of thieves and bad characters; and almost broke his mother's heart."

The character of Nancy was a type used by Dickens in several books: the teen-age prostitute whom fate had brought to a sad state but in whom there remained some basic goodness. A counterpart is found in the young prostitute Martha Endell in *David Copperfield*, who was instrumental in helping David to find Little Em'ly. When Sikes starts to beat Oliver upon his return, Nancy intervenes, saying: "I won't stand by and see it done, Fagin. You've got the boy, and what more would you have? Let him be—let him be—or I shall put the mark on some of you, that will bring me to the gallows before my time. . . . I thieved for you when I was a child not half as old as this. I have been in the same trade and the same service for twelve years since . . . It is my living; and the cold, wet, dirty streets are my home; and you're the wretch that drove me to them long ago, and that'll keep me there, day and night, day and night, until I die."

Dickens said that he was criticized for inconsistencies in the character of Nancy. The loyalty of her love for the villainous Sikes and her ultimate sacrifice of herself to save Oliver were not natural in a thieving, whoring, slut of the streets. Of such criticism Dickens commented: "It is useless to discuss whether the conduct and character of this girl seem natural or unnatural, probable or improbable, right or wrong.

IT IS TRUE. Every man who has watched these melancholy shades of life must know it to be so. From the first introduction of that poor wretch, to her laying her blood-stained head upon the robber's breast, there is not a word exaggerated or over-wrought. It is emphatically God's truth, for it is the truth He leaves in such depraved and miserable breasts; the hope yet lingering there; the last fair drop of water at the bottom of the week-choked well. It involves the best and the worst shades of our nature, much of its ugliest hues, and something of its most beautiful; it is a contradiction, an anomaly, an apparent impossibility; but it is the truth. I am glad to have had it doubted, for in that circumstance I should find a sufficient assurance (if I wanted any) that it needed to be told." Dickens would never tolerate any criticism of the lifelikeness of his youthful characters. They were not, he seemed to say, creations of his own imagination, but rather incarnations of real people reacting in the manner of living human beings. And, in most cases, this was true.

The exceptions, in the main, were his saintly young ladies who were at times too good to be true. One such makes an appearance in *Oliver Twist* shortly after the boy is returned to Fagin. This is seventeen-year-old Rose Maylie who, with her aunt, is the second benefactor of young Oliver. When she is first introduced Dickens describes her as she sits with her aunt: "The younger lady was in the lovely bloom and springtime of womanhood; at that age, when, if ever angels be for God's good purposes enthroned in mortal forms, they may be, without impiety, supposed to abide in such as hers. She was not past seventeen. Cast in so slight and exquisite a mould, so mild and gentle, so pure and beautiful, that earth seemed not her element, nor its rough creatures her fit companions. The very intelligence that shone in her deep blue eyes, and was stamped upon her noble head, seemed scarcely of her age, or of the world; and yet the changing expression of sweetness and good humour, the thousand lights that played about the face, and left no shadow there; above all, the smile, the cheerful, happy smile, were made for home, and fireside peace and happiness."

The paths of Rose and Oliver cross as the result of an attempted burglary of the Maylie home on which Oliver was forced to accompany Sikes and another thief, Toby, who said on his first sight of Oliver: "Fagin's eh! Wot an inwalable boy that'll make for the old ladies' pockets in chapel. His mug is a fortin' to him." The burglary misfired when Oliver was wounded by a shot from a servant's pistol. Deserted by his companions in a ditch when he loses consciousness, Oliver is captured by the Maylie menservants and put to bed in the Maylie home, where Rose immediately becomes his champion. When the family doctor assures her that "crime, like death, takes up her abode in many temples; and who can say that a fair outside shall not enshrine her?" Rose retorts with a spirited defense of the boy.

"But even if he has been wicked, think how young he is; think that he may never have known a mother's love, or the comfort of a home; that ill-usage and blows, or the want of bread, may have driven him to herd with men who have forced him to guilt. Aunt, dear aunt, for mercy's sake, think of this before you let them drag this sick child to a prison, which in any case must be the grave of all his chances of amendment. Oh! as you love me, and know that I have never felt the want of parents in your goodness and affection, but that I might have done so, and might have been equally helpless and unprotected with this poor child, have pity upon him before it is too late." And Dickens adds: "Oliver's pillow was smoothed by gentle hands that night, and loveliness and virtue watched him as he slept. He felt calm and happy and could have died without a murmur."

So a new life starts for Oliver that continues for many months in the Maylie home, a summer country cottage, and a hotel in London. Like his previous period with old Mr. Brownlow, this is a time of bliss for Oliver, with clean clothes, kind companionship, good books, and the other accessories of a fine home. This idyllic existence is threatened when his half brother Monks discovers him. Monks had already paid Fagin to make a thief of Oliver, an inducement that the fence scarcely needed. Now the brother returns to the old man with further nefarious plans to "bring down the boast of his father's will, by driving him through every jail in town, and then hauling him up for some capital felony which Fagin could manage, after making a good profit of him besides." Fortunately for Oliver, Nancy eavesdrops on this conversation between Monks and Fagin.

Determined to save Oliver from the fate planned by Monks, Nancy doses Sikes with laudanum and goes to call on Rose at the London hotel where the Maylie's are staying. The confrontation of the two seventeen-year-olds, the saintly, innocent Rose and the guttersnipe prostitute Nancy, is one of the most melodramatic incidents in the novel. Nancy identifies herself as the girl who "dragged little Oliver back to old Fagin's, on the night he went out from the house in Pentonville. I am the infamous creature you have heard of, that lives among the thieves, and that never from the first moment I can recollect my eyes and senses opening on London streets have known any better life, or kinder words than they have given me, so help me God! Do not mind shrinking from me, lady. I am younger than you would think, to look at me, but I am well used to it. The poorest women fall back as I make my way along the crowded pavement." When Rose speaks to her in tones of sympathy and offers help, Nancy tearfully replies: "Oh! lady, lady! If there were more like you there would be fewer like me." To keep Rose posted on further developments Nancy promises to walk on London Bridge every Sunday night between eleven and twelve, where Rose may contact her.

Rose does not know how to thwart Monks' and Fagin's villainous plans, until Oliver sees Mr. Brownlow in the street and follows him to his new home. Here Rose calls on him. Oliver and the old man are reunited, and Mr. Brownlow forms a coalition with the Maylies to save Oliver.

At this point Noah Claypole, the charity boy from Oliver's days with the undertaker, returns to the tale. Accompanied by the moronic servant girl Charlotte, Noah comes to London, after emptying Mr. Sowerberry's till, and falls in with Fagin. The country lout has big plans to become a gentleman and to make his paramour a lady through activities involving "pockets, women's redicules, houses, mail-coaches, banks." He admits that he will need some guidance in this and when Fagin offers to give him a start he asks: "What do you think would suit me now? Something not too trying for the strength, and not very dangerous, you know. That's the sort of thing." When Fagin suggests snatching bags and parcels from old ladies, Noah protests: "Don't they holler out a good deal and scratch sometimes? Ain't there any other line open?" They finally agree that the safest place for the boy to start is with the kinchin lay. "The kinchins, my dear," explains Fagin, "is the young children that's sent on errands by their mothers, with sixpences and shillings; and the lay is just to take the money away—they've always got it ready in their hands—and then knock them into the kennel and walk off very slow, as if there were nothing else matter, but a child fallen down and hurt itself. Ha! Ha! Ha!"

But Fagin has one special job for Noah. Nancy had tried to get out of the house on Sunday night and was restrained by Bill Sikes. The next Sunday Bill is out on a job and Fagin sets Noah to watch Nancy. The country boy follows her to London Bridge, where close to midnight she meets Rose and Mr. Brownlow and tells them where Monks may be found. She refuses their offer of protection for herself, saying: "You can do nothing to help me. I am past all help, indeed. . . . I am chained to my old life. I loathe and hate it now, but I cannot leave it." When Rose tries to press a purse of money upon her she pushes it aside. "I have not done this for money. Let me have that to think of. And yet—give me something you have worn: I should like to have something—no, no, not a ring—your gloves or handkerchief—anything that I can keep, as having belonged to you, sweet lady. There. God bless you. Good-night, good-night."

Noah overhears all this and reports it to Fagin, who in turn tells Sikes. The robber flies into a rage and vows to kill Nancy. Late in life Dickens commanded capacity audiences in England and the United States for lectures of readings from his works. A favorite passage, with him and the audience, was his dramatic re-enactment of the murder of Nancy. His son Charley later told of one day hearing screams and a scuffle in the garden at the Dickens' home at Gad's Hill. Going to investigate he found his father at the bottom of the garden rehearsing the murder scene and with fearful vehemence reproducing Bill's curses, Nancy's screams, and the blows that beat the girl to death. As Dickens' health failed, his physician tried to restrain him from doing this strenuous re-enactment, but the author, who had long fancied himself as an actor, refused to keep it from his public. The scene was described in *Oliver Twist* as follows, after Bill drew back the curtain of Nancy's bed:

"The girl was lying, half dressed, upon it. He had roused her from sleep, for she raised herself with a hurried and startled look.

" 'Get up!' said the man.

" 'It *is* you, Bill!' said the girl, with an expression of pleasure at his return.

" 'It is' was the reply. 'Get up.'

"There was a candle burning, but the man hastily drew it from the candlestick, and hurled it under the grate. Seeing the faint light of early day without, the girl rose to undraw the curtain.

" 'Let it be,' said Sikes, thrusting his hand before her. 'There's light enough for wot I've got to do.'

" 'Bill,' said the girl, in the low voice of alarm, 'why do you look like that at me!'

"The robber sat regarding her, for a few seconds, with dilated nostrils and heaving breast; and then, grasping her by the head and throat, dragged her into the middle of the room, and looking once towards the door, placed his heavy hand upon her mouth.

" 'Bill, Bill!' gasped the girl, wrestling with the strength of mortal fear—'I—I won't scream or cry—not once—hear me—speak to me—tell me what I have done!'

" 'You know, you she devil!' returned the robber, suppressing his breath. 'You were watched tonight; every word you said was heard.'

" 'Then spare my life for the love of Heaven, as I spared yours,' rejoined the girl, clinging to him. 'Bill, dear Bill, you

Monmouth Street. (*Sketches by Boz*) Page 6.

My magnificent order at the public-house. (*David Copperfield*) Page 36.

I make myself known to my aunt. (*David Copperfield*) Page 40.

Oliver asking for more.
(*Oliver Twist*)
Page 66.

Oliver plucks up a spirit.
(*Oliver Twist*)
Page 71.

Oliver's reception by Fagin and the boys. (*Oliver Twist*) Page 74.

A rest by the way. (*Old Curiosity Shop*) Page 93.

Mrs. Jarley's Wax Works. (*Old Curiosity Shop*) Page 96.

The pensioner entertainment. (*Little Dorrit*) Page 110.

Nicholas congratulates Arthur Gride on his wedding morning.
(*Nicholas Nickleby*) Page 115.

The Dombey family.
(*Dombey and Son*)
Page 116.

Paul and Mrs. Pipchin.
(*Dombey and Son*)
Page 129.

The internal economy
of Dotheboys Hall.
(*Nicholas Nickleby*)
Page 142.

The breaking-up at
Dotheboys Hall.
(*Nicholas Nickleby*)
Page 146.

Polly rescues the Charitable Grinder. (*Dombey and Son*) Page 149.

Doctor Blimber's young gentlemen as they appeared when enjoying themselves. (*Dombey and Son*) Page 151.

A quiet game of cribbage. (*Old Curiosity Shop*) Page 171.

The terrible stranger
in the churchyard.
(*Great Expectations*)
Page 187.

Trabb's boy.
(*Great Expectations*)
Page 194.

Miss Tox pays a visit to the Toodle family. (*Dombey and Son*) Page 198.

Nicholas engaged as tutor
in a private family.
(*Nicholas Nickleby*)
Page 199.

The Tetterby family.
(*The Haunted Man*)
Page 220.

cannot have the heart to kill me. Oh! think of all I have given up, only this one night, for you. You *shall* have time to think, and save yourself this crime. I will not loose my hold; you cannot throw me off. Bill, Bill, for dear God's sake, for your own, for mine, stop before you spill my blood! I have been true to you, upon my guilty soul I have!'

"The man struggled violently to release his arms; but those of the girl were clasped round his, and tear as he would, he could not tear them away.

" 'Bill,' cried the girl, striving to lay her head upon his breast, 'the gentleman, and that dear lady, told me to-night of a home in some foreign country where I could end my days in solitude and peace. Let me see them again, and beg them, on my knees, to show the same mercy and goodness to you; and let us both leave this dreadful place, and far apart lead better lives, and forget how we have lived, except in prayers, and never see each other more. It is never too late to repent. They told me so—I feel it now—but we must have time—a little, little time!'

"The housebreaker freed one arm, and grasped his pistol. The certainty of immediate detection if he fired flashed across his mind, even in the midst of his fury; and he beat it twice, with all the force he could summon, upon the upturned face that almost touched his own.

"She staggered and fell, nearly blinded with the blood that rained down from a deep gash in her forehead; but raising herself, with difficulty, on her knees, drew from her bosom a white handkerchief—Rose Maylie's own—and holding it up in her folded hands, as high towards Heaven as her feeble strength would allow, breathed one prayer for mercy to her Maker.

"It was a ghastly figure to look upon. The murderer, staggering backwards to the wall, and shutting out the sight with his hand, seized a heavy club and struck her down."

From this point the action of the novel moves rapidly to a close, with little emphasis on its juvenile principal. The villains, of course, all get their just deserts. Sikes inadvertently hangs himself while trying to escape the law. Fagin is tried and condemned to be hung. Monks is forced to tell all by Mr. Brownlow and then permitted to depart for the United States, where he dies in prison. The Artful Dodger is taken and transported for life. The heroic characters receive their rewards. Rose, whom Monks has disclosed as the younger sister of Oliver's mother and merely an adopted niece of Mrs. Maylie, marries her foster aunt's young son, a minister. Oliver is adopted by Mr. Brownlow. "Removing with him and the old housekeeper to within a mile of the parsonage-house, where his dear friends resided, he gratified the only remaining wish of Oliver's warm and earnest heart, and thus linked together a little society, whose condition approached as nearly to one of perfect happiness as can ever be known in this changing world."

CHAPTER

IV

SOME SAINTLY MAIDENS

If a medal were given for goodness—like Uriah Heep's for 'umbleness—there are several young ladies in Dickens' novels who surely would be in the finals for the award in a competition with virtuous females in all the world's literature. These are the saintly maidens who are principal juvenile characters in many of his novels. They are, perhaps, the least lifelike of all the author's young people because no one ever knew a living girl who was so thoroughly good. They are symbolic rather than real; symbolic of purity, virtue, innocence, self-sacrifice, and all of the highest ideals of angelic womanhood. They stand on pedestals high above the human race and their creator demands that they be worshipped. As mentioned earlier in this volume, most Dickens experts relate them to the author's sixteen-year-old sister-in-law, Mary Hogarth.

In making the final award of the goodness medal it would be difficult to select a winner from at least six of Dickens' girls. Should it go to Rose Maylie in *Oliver Twist*, to Made-

line Bray in *Nicholas Nickleby*, to Florence Dombey in
Dombey and Son, to Agnes Wickfield in *David Copperfield*,
to Little Dorrit in the novel of that name, to Little Nell in
Old Curiosity Shop? Supporters of any one of these virtuous
young ladies can make a case that she is the ultimate paragon
and can present valid evidence to support it. But the majority
of Dickensians seem to feel that the award probably should
go to Little Nell, if only because she not only lived, but died,
as a model of faultless self-sacrifice.

The novel *Old Curiosity Shop* opens in a somewhat unusual manner in that the story is told, for the first three chapters, by an old man who is an anonymous narrator and who
then disappears from the book. This kindly person meets
thirteen-year-old Nell when she asks him, on a London
street, how to get to her home, a rather distant address. He
offers to guide her there and the first inkling of Nell's character is his remark that, as she put her hand in his, she rather
seemed "to lead and take care of me than I to be protecting
her."

The child's home is the old curiosity shop of the title—a
place full of "old and curious things which seem to crouch
in odd corners of this town, and to hide their musty treasures
from the public eye in jealousy and distrust. There were suits
of mail standing like ghosts in armour, here and there; fantastic carvings brought from monkish cloisters; rusty weapons
of various kinds; distorted figures in china, and wood, and
iron, and ivory; tapestry, and strange furniture that might
have been designed in dreams." Although the book is named
for it, the shop plays no important part in the story and is
dropped after the first few chapters.

Here the unknown stranger meets the orphan girl's grandfather, with whom she lives. He is moved by the contrast

between the aged man and the young girl, and by her obvious love and concern for her grandfather. He remarks: "It was pleasant to observe the fresh flowers in the room, the pet bird with a green bough shading his little cage, the breath of freshness and youth which seemed to rustle through the old dull house and hover round the child. It was curious, but not so pleasant, to turn from the beauty and grace of the girl, to see the stooping figure, careworn face, and jaded aspect of the old man. As he grew weaker and more feeble, what would become of this lovely little creature; poor protector as he was, say that he died—what would her fate be then?"

The anonymous narrator also serves to introduce several other characters who are principals in the story. There is Kit Nubbles, a shock-headed, shambling, awkward lad slightly older than Nell, with an uncommonly wide mouth, red cheeks, a very turned-up nose, and a peculiarly comical expression of face. Kit works as an errand boy for Nell's grandfather and is in love with the little girl. There is Fred, Nell's no-good older brother, and his friend Dick Swiveller, a rather engaging ne're-do-well lawyer's clerk who makes his first appearance with a terrible hangover. And there is Daniel Quilp, one of Dickens' slimier villains. Quilp was "so low in stature as to be quite a dwarf; though his head and face were large enough for the body of a giant. His black eyes were restless, sly, and cunning; his mouth and chin bristly with the stubble of a coarse, hard beard; and his complexion was one of that kind which never looks clean or wholesome. But what added most to the grotesque expression of his face was a ghastly smile, which, appearing to be the mere result of habit, and to have no connection with any mirthful or complacent feeling, constantly revealed the few discolored fangs that were yet scattered in his mouth, and gave him the aspect of a panting dog."

Nell's life is centered solely on caring for her grandfather. When the story opens she is very disturbed because of the old man's mysterious conduct. He leaves the house late at night, not to return until shortly before dawn. And he has something to do with the ugly Quilp; Nell is sometimes sent across the city with messages for the dwarf, who is also a frequent visitor at the shop. In former days "she had gone singing through the dim rooms, and moving with gay and lightsome step among their dusty treasures, making them older by her young life, and sterner and more grim by her gay and cheerful presence." But now she lives in constant fear.

"It was not the monotonous days unchequered by variety and uncheered by pleasant companionship, it was not the dark dreary evenings or the long solitary nights, it was not the absence of every slight and easy pleasure for which young hearts beat high, or the knowing nothing of childhood but its weakness and its easily wounded spirit, that had wrung such tears from Nell. To see the old man struck down beneath the pressure of some hidden grief, to mark his wavering and unsettled state, to be agitated at times with a dreadful fear that his mind was wandering, and to trace in his words and looks the dawning of despondent madness; to watch and wait and listen for confirmation of these things day after day, and to feel and know that, come what might, they were alone in the world with no one to help or advise or care about them—these were causes of depression and anxiety that might have sat heavily on an older breast, with many influences at work to cheer and gladden it, but how heavily on the mind of a young child to whom they were ever present, and who was constantly surrounded by all that could keep such thoughts in restless action!"

Evil machinations surround Nell. Her brother Fred, believing that the grandfather has a hidden store of wealth, proposes that his friend Dick Swiveller marry her. By a "very little coaxing and threatening" the brother is sure that he can bend her to his will. Dick protests that she is but "nearly fourteen," but Fred says that it can wait two or three years—"the old man does not look a long liver."

Quilp, too, has leering eyes on the child. On a visit to the shop he has the grandfather send Nell from the room and then torments him with his lascivious interest in the girl as the old man kisses her before she leaves. " 'Ah!' said the dwarf, smacking his lips, 'what a nice kiss that was—just upon the rosy part. What a capital kiss!' . . . 'Such a fresh, blooming, modest little bud, neighbour' said Quilp, nursing his short leg, and making his eyes twinkle very much, 'such a chubby, rosy, cozy, little Nell!'

" 'She's so . . . small, so compact, so beautifully modelled, so fair, with such blue veins and such a transparent skin, and such little feet, and such winning ways—but bless me, you're nervous! Why neighbour, what's the matter?' " The monster also proposes to the child that she " 'be Mrs. Quilp the second, when Mrs. Quilp the first is dead, sweet Nell. . . . to be my wife, my little cherry-cheeked, red-lipped wife . . .' "

Despite Fred's opinion that his grandfather has a hidden fortune, the old man protests that he is very poor. But he reiterates that he is going to do something that will make fine financial provision for Little Nell. It turns out that he is a compulsive gambler. The secret of his nightly expeditions, during which Nell waits through the dark by the window for him to return, is that he is out gambling—and losing. Getting money with which to gamble is the basis of his association with Quilp, to whom he has mortgaged everything he owns.

When Quilp finally refuses to advance him any more money, the old man breaks down and is desperately ill. Quilp moves in, shutters up the shop, and relegates Nell and her grandfather to an upper room. As the grandfather mends, Nell proposes that they steal away and be beggars: "I have no fear but we shall have enough, I am sure we shall. Let us walk through country places, and sleep in fields and under trees, and never think of money again, or anything that can make you sad, but rest at nights, and have the sun and wind upon our faces in the day, and thank God together!" When the old man is strong enough they put this plan into execution, leaving the house stealthily just before dawn. "Forth from the city, while it yet slumbered, went the two poor adventurers, wandering they knew not whither."

The main theme of the remainder of the book is the wanderings of the child and the old man. There are subthemes, of course, as in all Dickens' novels. Kit goes to work for a nice man named Garland, where there is a young servant girl named Barbara. With the aid of his lawyer, Sampson Brass, Quilp plants some money on Kit and has him convicted of theft and sent to jail. He is subsequently vindicated through the efforts of Swiveller, Garland, a noble notary, and a stranger who is seeking Nell and her grandfather and who turns out to be the old man's younger brother. Kit ultimately marries Barbara. There is an amusing substory involving Dick Swiveller and another thirteen-year-old orphan girl who is a servant of the Brass's. She has no name and Dick calls her the Marchioness. This ends by Dick mending his ways, christening the girl Sophronia Sphynx, sending her to school and, six years later, marrying her.

But all of this is subordinate to the wanderings of Nell and her aged charge. On the first day they slowly make their way out of the city, the grandfather insisting that they go "farther, farther." They finally reach the green fields which remind Nell of pictures in *Pilgrim's Progress*, which they had looked at together. " 'I feel as if we were both Christian,' she says, 'and laid down on this grass all the cares and troubles we brought with us, never to take them up again.' " As they pause to rest and refresh themselves by a stream, Nell washes her grandfather and dries him "with her simple dress." The relationship between the two is again made evident by the words of the old man:

" 'I can do nothing for myself, my darling,' said the grandfather. 'I don't know how it is, I could once, but the time's gone. Don't leave me, Nell; say that thou'lt not leave me. I loved thee all the while, indeed I did. If I lose thee too, my dear, I must die!'

"He laid his head upon her shoulder and moaned piteously. The time had been, and a very few days before, when the child could not have restrained her tears and must have wept with him. But now she soothed him with gentle and tender words, smiled at his thinking they could ever part, and rallied him cheerfully upon the jest. He was soon calmed and fell asleep, singing to himself in a low voice, like a little child."

Toward the end of their first day the pair fall in with a traveling marionette show operated by two men, Mr. Codlin and Mr. Short. These two have stopped by the road to make repairs on their puppets and Nell helps by neatly sewing the bedraggled clothes of Punch and Judy. The showmen suggest that Nell and her grandfather spend the night with them at a nearby public house. Nell has a little money, including one gold piece which, for safety's sake, she sews into her dress when she reaches the inn. At this establishment they are joined by assorted mountebanks: the Grinders, a father who plays the trumpet and his two children who are stilt-walkers; Jerry and his dancing dogs; a giant; a legless female dwarf, and a conjurer. All are on their way to perform at the races that are to take place the next day.

Nell and her grandfather go with them to the races, where Nell tries her hand at begging for the first time by gathering some field flowers which she tries to sell to well-dressed ladies in carriages. Some of these ladies notice the child and say: " 'See what a pretty face!' " But "they let the pretty face pass on, and never thought that it looked tired and hungry." Nell meanwhile has become suspicious of Codlin, who insists that he is their true friend and that they should keep close to him. Actually, Codlin believes that friends or relations might pay a reward for information about this ill-assorted pair and he intends to turn them in to the first magistrate. Nell thwarts him by sneaking away with her grandfather while the pair are putting on their show.

The grandfather is beset by apprehensions that they are being hunted; that if they are taken he will be separated from Nell and confined in an institution. Briefly, his terrors communicate themselves to the child. "In one so young, and so unused to the scenes in which she had lately moved, this sinking of the spirit was not surprising. But Nature often enshrines gallant and noble hearts in weak bosoms—oftenest, God bless her, in female breasts—and when the child, casting her tearful eyes upon the old man, remembered how weak he was, and how destitute and helpless he would be if she failed him, her heart swelled within her, and animated her with new strength and fortitude. 'We are quite safe now, and have nothing to fear indeed, dear grandfather,' she said."

Late in this day they come to a small village where they meet an old schoolmaster, Mr. Marton, puttering in his garden. This kindly soul offers them shelter in his cottage-schoolhouse. The schoolmaster is distraught because his best and favorite pupil is very ill. This unnamed youngster is apparently introduced into the story—as are some other children in Dickens' writing—solely to provide a youthful deathbed scene. This victim is "a very young boy; quite a little child. His hair still hung in curls about his face, and his eyes were very bright; but their light was of Heaven, not earth." When he sees Nell, whom the schoolmaster has taken to visit him, he asks: "Who is that? I am afraid to kiss her, lest I should make her ill. Ask her to shake hands with me."

The schoolmaster reminds the dying child of the garden and tells him: " 'You must make haste to visit it again, for I think the very flowers have missed you, and are less gay than they used to be. You will come soon, my dear, very soon now —won't you?' . . . In the silence that ensued, the hum of distant voices borne upon the evening air came floating through the open window. 'What's that?' said the sick child, opening his eyes.

" 'The boys at play upon the green.'

"He took a handkerchief from his pillow and tried to wave it above his head. But the feeble arm dropped powerless down.

" 'Shall I do it?' said the schoolmaster.

" 'Please wave it at the window,' was the faint reply. 'Tie it to the lattice. Some of them may see it there. Perhaps they'll think of me, and look this way.'

"He raised his head, and glanced from the fluttering signal to his idle bat, that lay with slate and book and other boyish property upon a table in the room. And then he laid him softly down once more, and asked if the little girl were there, for he could not see her.

"She stepped forward, and pressed the passive hand that lay upon the coverlet. The two old friends and companions—for such they were, though they were man and child—held each other in a long embrace, and then the little scholar turned his face towards the wall, and fell asleep.

"The poor schoolmaster sat in the same place, holding the small cold hand in his, and chafing it. It was but the hand of a dead child. He felt that; and yet he chafed it still, and could not lay it down."

The next morning they leave the schoolmaster and wander on. Late this day they come upon a little caravan: "a smart little house on wheels, with white dimity curtains festooning the windows." This was the office wagon of Jarley's Wax Works and the traveling home of its proprietor, Mrs. Jarley. This worthy woman gives them tea and carries them on in her caravan, questioning Nell curiously as to their circumstances. She is appalled when she finds that the child is wandering the roads with no home and no destination and offers her a job. When Nell protests that she has her grandfather to take care of, Mrs. Jarley tartly avers that he seems old enough to take care of himself, if he ever will be. Nell replies: " 'But he never will be, I fear he never will be again. Pray do not speak harshly to him. We are very thankful to you,' she added . . . ; 'but neither of us could part from the other if all the wealth of the world were halved between us.' " So kindly Mrs. Jarley offers them both jobs; the old man can dust the wax figures and make himself generally useful and the child can learn to escort visitors through the display and explain each of the exhibits.

This happy situation continues for several days. Then, one

evening, Nell and her grandfather take a long walk out of
the town in which the wax works is exhibiting, are caught in
a tremendous storm and forced to spend the night at an inn.
Here some men are playing cards and the grandfather's mania
overcomes him. "The child saw with astonishment and alarm
that his whole appearance had undergone a complete change.
His face was flushed and eager, his eyes were strained, his
teeth set, his breath came short and thick, and the hand he
laid upon her arm trembled so violently that she shook beneath its grasp."

The old man insists that Nell give him all the money that
they have, which she reluctantly does except for the hidden
gold piece. After he loses it she has to change the gold piece
to pay for the lodgings. As she does so she thinks she sees a
figure slinking in the hall, watching. Later, she lies in bed
consumed with fear of the strange surroundings, the "very
ill-looking" men with whom her grandfather had gambled,
and the figure she had seen sneaking through the passage
downstairs. "At last sleep gradually stole upon her—a broken,
fitful sleep, troubled by dreams of falling from high towers,
and waking with a start and in great terror. A deeper slumber
followed this—and then—What! That figure in the room.

"A figure was there. Yes, she had drawn up the blind to
admit the light when it should be dawn, and there, between
the foot of the bed and the dark casement, it crouched and
slunk along, groping its way with noiseless hands, and stealing round the bed. She had no voice to cry for help, no
power to move, but lay still, watching it.

"On it came—on, silently and stealthily, to the bed's head.
The breath so near her pillow, that she shrunk back into it,
lest those wandering hands should light upon her face. Back
again it stole to the window—then turned its head towards

her." The figure was that of her grandfather, who had come to steal the change from the gold piece.

From that night on the old man took all the money that they made at the wax works and returned to his nightly gambling expeditions. Made sleepless by worry, Nell takes long walks at night and on one such she comes upon a gypsy caravan where her grandfather and the men whom he gambled with at the inn have just finished playing. The old man has lost his small stake and is moaning that the lack of sufficient funds prevents him from playing long enough to make the killing that he knows is in the offing. Nell hears his two companions incite him to rob Mrs. Jarley, and the grandfather agrees to do so the next night.

Nell follows the old man back to the caravan and starts to prepare for bed. "But who could sleep—sleep! who could lie passively down, distracted by such terrors? They came upon her more and more strongly yet." Half undressed, she runs to her grandfather's bed in the wagon and tells him that she has had "a dreadful, horrible dream"—a dream of "grey-haired men like you, in darkened rooms by night, robbing sleepers of their gold." They must fly, at once. "Nothing but flight can save us." So the pair again take to the road before dawn. "In the pale moonlight, which lent a wanness of its own to the delicate face where thoughtful care already mingled with the winning grace and loveliness of youth, the too bright eye, the spiritual head, the lips that pressed each other with such high resolve and courage of the heart, the slight figure firm in its bearing and yet so very weak, told their silent tale; but told it only to the wind that rustled by, which, taking up its burden, carried, perhaps to some mother's pillow, faint dreams of childhood fading in its bloom, and resting in the sleep that knows no waking."

The next two days are spent on a canal boat, the operators of which offer them a lift. Nell uses her last pennies to buy food at a stop where the boatmen buy some beer and then spends a harrowing night coping with the drunken boatmen, who insist that she sing for them throughout the night. On the second evening they are dropped in the middle of a large industrial town. It is raining, they have no funds for lodgings or food, and Nell decides that they will sleep in a doorway. As they start to settle down a frightening, smoke-blackened man comes from the house and, after learning their dire straits, tells them that he can give them a warm place to spend the night on the ashes in the iron foundry in which he works. To Nell the warm ashes seem as a bed of down, and the good Samaritan shares his meager breakfast with them in the morning and presses two smoke-grimed pennies in the child's hand as they leave.

On they limp through the squalid industrial area, seeking the green country beyond. When their two pennies are gone the child tries to beg, but the people are too poor. They have had nothing to eat for a day when Nell sees a figure before them that she thinks she recognizes. When she catches up to the other traveler it proves to be Mr. Marton, the old schoolmaster. The child falls senseless at his feet and the schoolmaster carries her to a nearby inn. When she has been revived and fed, Mr. Marton explains that he has secured a new post in a village some distance ahead and offers to take Nell and her grandfather with him. They travel on in a wagon to their ultimate destination.

This is the end of Nell's wanderings. The village to which Mr. Marton has been appointed proves to be very, very old and very quiet. There is an ancient ivy-covered stone church and hard by it a small schoolhouse. After visiting the authorities Mr. Marton returns and tells Nell that he has secured for her and her grandfather a house next to his. An old man who used to show visitors through the church has died and Nell and her charge may have his very old two-room house and a small stipend for performing this service. The couple settle down, finally, to peace. Everybody is very poor, but very kind. Nell busies herself mending the tattered hangings of their home and the church and she and her grandfather plan to make a garden spot of the churchyard, starting with the graves of children. The neighbors bring them small gifts and Nell becomes a favorite of the children of the village, particularly the small son of the old sexton. This child seems to have visions and the first intimation of Nell's impending death is given in a conversation with the little boy.

"It happened, that, as she was reading in the old spot by herself one day, this child came running in with his eyes full of tears, and after holding her from him, and looking at her eagerly for a moment, clasped his little arms passionately about her neck.

" 'What now?' said Nell, soothing him. 'What is the matter?'

" 'She is not one yet!' cried the boy, embracing her still more closely. 'No, no. Not yet.'

"She looked at him wonderingly, and putting his hair back from his face, and kissing him, asked what he meant.

" 'You must not be one, dear Nell,' cried the boy. 'We can't see them. They never come to play with us, or talk to us. Be what you are. You are better so.'

" 'I do not understand you,' said the child. 'Tell me what you mean.'

" 'Why, they say,' replied the boy, looking up into her face, 'that you will be an Angel, before the birds sing again.

But you won't be, will you? Don't leave us, Nell, though the sky is bright. Do not leave us!'

"The child dropped her head, and put her hands before her face.

" 'She cannot bear the thought!' cried the boy, exulting through his tears. 'You will not go. You know how sorry we should be. Dear Nell, tell me that you'll stay amongst us. Oh! Pray, pray, tell me that you will.'

"The little creature folded his hands, and knelt down at her feet.

" 'Only look at me, Nell,' said the boy, 'and tell me that you'll stop, and then I shall know that they are wrong, and will cry no more. Won't you say yes, Nell?'

"Still the drooping head and hidden face, and the child quite silent—save for her sobs.

" 'After a time,' pursued the boy, trying to draw away her hand, 'the kind angels will be glad to think that you are not among them, and that you stayed here to be with us. Willy went away, to join them; but if he had known how I should miss him in our little bed at night, he never would have left me, I am sure.'

"Yet the child could make him no answer, and sobbed as though her heart were bursting."

Meanwhile, in far-off London, the stranger who is not yet disclosed as the grandfather's younger brother has learned where the wanderers have settled. With Kit and the boy's benefactor, Mr. Garland, he hastens to the village in a chaise. They arrive at night to find the grandfather huddled over the fire. Nell, he says, is asleep in the other room, they must not wake her. " 'She is sleeping soundly,' he said; 'but no wonder. Angel hands have strewn the ground deep with snow, that the lightest footstep may be lighter yet; and the very birds are dead, that they may not wake her. She used to feed them, sir. Though ever so cold and hungry, the timid things would fly from us. They never flew from her!' . . . 'Why dost thou lie so idle there, dear Nell,' he murmured, 'when there are bright red berries out of doors waiting for thee to pluck them! Why dost thou lie so idle there, when thy little friends come creeping to the door, crying "Where is Nell—sweet Nell?"—and sob, and weep, because they do not see thee! She was always gentle with children. The wildest would do her bidding—she had a tender way with them, indeed she had!' "

The old man does not recognize Kit nor understand his brother's avowal of their relationship. He is fearful that the visitors have come to take him away from the child—"You plot among you to wean my heart from her." Trembling, and holding the lamp before him, he totters toward the other room.

"Waving them off with his hand, and calling softly to her as he went, he stole into the room. They who were left behind drew close together, and after a few whispered words—not unbroken by emotion, or easily uttered—followed him. They moved so gently that their footsteps made no noise; but there were sobs from among the group, and sounds of grief and mourning.

"For she was dead. There, upon her little bed, she lay at rest. The solemn stillness was no marvel now.

"She was dead. No sleep so beautiful and calm, so free from trace of pain, so fair to look upon. She seemed a creature fresh from the hand of God, and waiting for the breath of life; not one who had lived and suffered death.

"Her couch was dressed with here and there some winter berries and green leaves, gathered in a spot she had been used to favour. 'When I die, put near me something that has loved the light, and had the sky above it always.' Those were her words.

"She was dead. Dear, gentle, patient, noble Nell was dead. Her little bird—a poor slight thing the pressure of a finger would have crushed—was stirring nimbly in its cage; and the strong heart of its child mistress was mute and motionless forever.

"Where were the traces of her early cares, her sufferings, and fatigues? All gone. Sorrow was dead indeed in her, but peace and perfect happiness were born; imaged in her tranquil beauty and profound repose.

"And still her former self lay there, unaltered in this change. Yes. The old fireside has smiled upon that same sweet face; it has passed, like a dream, through haunts of misery and care; at the door of the poor schoolmaster on the summer evening, before the furnace fire upon the cold wet night, at the still bedside of the dying boy, there had been the same mild lovely look. So shall we know the angels in their majesty, after death."

So died Little Nell, perhaps the saintliest of all Dickens' saintly maidens. Learned critics, then and since, have for the most part felt that the child was unbelievable in her sanctity. When she died her creator wept bitterly and, in those Victorian days when emotional expression was not considered shameful, many of the literate common people of the English-speaking world wept with him.

As a grandfather was Little Nell's cross, a father was Little Dorrit's. This character, around whom the novel of that name is built, is usually thought of as one of Dickens' juvenile creations, principally because of the "little" in the name, and the fact that she looked like a twelve- or thirteen-year-old girl. In fact, throughout most of the novel, she is in her twenties. She is twenty-two when she is first introduced, working for a Mrs. Clennam. "Little Dorrit let herself out to do needlework. At so much a day—or so little—from eight to eight, Little Dorrit was to be hired. Punctual to the moment, Little Dorrit appeared; punctual to the moment, Little Dorrit vanished. What became of Little Dorrit between the two eights, was a mystery. . . .

"It was not easy to make out Little Dorrit's face; she was so retiring, plied her needle in such removed corners, and started away so scared if encountered on the stairs. But it seemed to be a pale transparent face, quick in expression, though not beautiful in feature, its soft hazel eyes excepted. A delicately bent head, a fine form, a quick little pair of busy hands, and a shabby dress—it must needs have been very shabby to look at all so, being so neat—were Little Dorrit as she sat at work."

Little Dorrit's character is established in a long flash back that deals with her childhood. Twenty-two years before the story begins, a debtor, William Dorrit, had been confined to the Marshalsea prison. "He was a shy, retiring man; well-looking, though in an effeminate style; with a mild voice, curling hair, and irresolute hands—rings upon the fingers in those days—which nervously wandered to his trembling lip a hundred times, in the first half-hour of his acquaintance with the jail."

Dorrit's troubles were caused by the failure of a partnership in which one partner had defaulted. Dorrit did not understand what had happened and was sure that he would be out of prison in a few days. Meanwhile, could the rules permit his wife and children to stay with him? " 'The children?' said the turnkey. 'And the rules? Why, lord set you up like a corner pin, we've a reg'lar playground o' children here. Children? Why, we swarm with 'em. How many a you got?'" The debtor had two offspring: Edward, called Tip, a child of three, and Fanny, aged two. Six months later a third child was born in the prison, Amy, called, because of her diminutive stature, Little Dorrit, and known throughout the prison, which would be her home for almost twenty-five years, as the Child of the Marshalsea, as her male parent came to be known, through his long tenure, as the Father of the Marshalsea.

As a very small child Little Dorrit was the pet of the "collegians" in the institution, "it being almost a part of the entrance footing of every new collegian to nurse the child who had been born in the college." In time she comes to realize that it is not normal to live in a prison. "At what period of her early life the little creature began to perceive that it was not the habit of all the world to live locked up in narrow yards surrounded by high walls with spikes at the top would be a difficult question to settle. But she was a very, very little creature indeed, when she had somehow gained the knowledge that her clasp of her father's hand was to be always loosened at the door which the great key opened; and that while her own light steps were free to pass beyond it, his feet must never cross that line. A pitiful and plaintive look, with which she had begun to regard him when she was still extremely young, was perhaps a part of this discovery."

The child's particular mentor was a turnkey, Bob, with whom she sat by the hour in a little chair that he had made for her. She pondered about the outside world and queried Bob regarding it.

"Wistful and wondering, she would sit in summer weather by the high fender in the Lodge, looking up at the sky through the barred window, until bars of light would arise, when she turned her eyes away, between her and her friend, and she would see him through a grating too.

" 'Thinking of the fields,' the turnkey said once, after watching her, 'ain't you?'

" 'Where are they?' she inquired.

" 'Why, they're—over there, my dear,' said the turnkey, with a vague flourish of his key. 'Just about there.'

" 'Does anybody open them, and shut them? Are they locked?'

"The turnkey was discomfited. 'Well!' said he. 'Not in general.'

" 'Are they very pretty, Bob?' She called him Bob by his own particular request and instruction.

" 'Lovely. Full of flowers. There's buttercups, and there's daisies, and there's—the turnkey hesitated, being short of floral nomenclature—'there's dandelions, and all manner of games.'

" 'Is it very pleasant to be there, Bob?'

" 'Prime,' said the turnkey.

" 'Was father every there?'

" 'Hem!' coughed the turnkey. 'O yes, he was there, some-times.'

" 'Is he sorry not to be there now?'

" 'N—not particular,' said the turnkey.

" 'Nor any of the people?' she asked, glancing at the listless crowd within. 'O are you quite sure and certain, Bob?' "

Mrs. Dorrit dies when her youngest child is eight years old and from that time Little Dorrit starts to take responsibility, not only for her father but for her wayward older sister and the brother who is already on the road of idleness and irre-sponsibility that will be his part in life. "What her pitiful look saw, at that early time, in her father, in her sister, in her brother, in the jail; how much or how little of the wretched truth it pleased God to make visible to her; lies hidden with many mysteries. It is enough that she was inspired to be something which was not what the rest were, and to be that something, different and laborious, for the sake of the rest. Inspired? Yes. Shall we speak of the inspiration of a poet or a priest, and not of the heart impelled by love and self-devotion to the lowliest work in the lowliest way of life!"

Mr. Dorrit has by now developed a manner of extreme dignity and concern for his gentility. He takes his position as Father of the Marshalsea very seriously and holds court for visitors, making it clear that he is willing to accept "testimonials" of their respect; in short, charitable contributions. But beneath this demeanor he is bewildered and completely ineffectual. At first, after the death of his wife, Little Dorrit can do little more than sit with him to provide comfort, but this he soon comes to need and expect. "Through this little gate she passed out of childhood into the care-laden world."

By the age of thirteen the child could read and keep simple accounts sufficiently well to manage the household budget. She had gotten her brother and sister sent to day schools outside the prison for short periods. Then, when a dancing master is incarcerated, she sees an opportunity to create a career for her sister Fanny. She has saved a little from her father's "testimonials" and approaches the new prisoner, saying, "If you please, I was born here, sir." The dancing master had heard of her, as had all new inmates when they came to the prison, and, impressed by the serious little figure with the great eyes who wanted nothing for herself but only help for her sister, he agrees to teach Fanny for nothing. The older daughter learns well and goes on to a career as a dancer. Little

Dorrit has no such high ambitions for herself, but when a seamstress joins the company the child importunes her for instruction and soon becomes a fine needlewoman.

Tip was a problem; he did not want to work. "With intervals of Marshalsea lounging . . . his small second mother, aided by her trusty friend (the turnkey), got him into a warehouse, into a market garden, into the hop trade, into the law again, into an auctioneer's, into a brewery, into a stockbroker's, into the law again, into a general dealer's, into a distillery, into the law again, into a wool house, into a dry-goods house, into the Billingsgate trade, into the foreign fruit trade, and into the docks. But whatever Tip went into, he came out of tired, announcing that he had cut it. Wherever he went, this foredoomed Tip appeared to take the prison walls with him, and to set them up in such trade or calling; and to prowl about within their narrow limits in the old slip-shod, purposeless, down-at-heel way; until the real immovable Marshalsea walls asserted their fascination over him, and brought him back."

Tip finally gets himself a job with a horse dealer and the next time he returns to the Marshalsea he is there as a debtor, in for forty pounds. In addition to all her other woes, Little Dorrit must conceal this fact from her father, as she has created a fiction that sister Fanny is not working as a dancer but is serving as a companion to an old uncle. It would be far beneath the dignity of the Father of the Marshalsea to have his children work, and to know that his son was a debtor would cause him inexpressible anguish. Little Dorrit builds a screen around him so that he may live contentedly with his false gentility, graciously accepting the "testimonials" which he thinks supports his family, while his youngest daughter

busily plies her needle for pay outside the walls during the
day and serves her parent at night.

During her childhood Little Dorrit has a suitor, John Chivery, the son of another turnkey who hoped, "in the fullness
of time, to leave him the inheritance of an unstained key; and
from his early youth familiarized him with the duties of the
office, and with an ambition to retain the prison-lock in the
family. . . . Years agone, when the object of his affections was
wont to sit in her little arm-chair by the high Lodge fender,
Young John (family name, Chivery), a year older than herself, had eyed her with admiring wonder. When he had
played with her in the yard, his favorite game had been to
counterfeit locking her up in corners, and to counterfeit let-
ting her out for real kisses. When he grew tall enough to
peep through the keyhole of the great lock of the main door,
he had divers times sat down his father's dinner, or supper,
to get on as it might on the outer side thereof, while he
stood taking cold in one eye by dint of peeping at her
through that airy perspective."

At the end of their adolescence Young John proclaims his
love, but Little Dorrit sends him away, begging him not to
speak of it again. There is no place in her self-sacrificing life
for love or marriage.

So ends the story of Little Dorrit as a juvenile, which is
encompassed in the first tenth of the novel. "Worldly wise in
hard and poor necessities, she was innocent in all things else.
Innocent, in the mist through which she saw her father, and
the prison, and the turbid living river that flowed through it
and flowed on." By this time the girl has come to the attention of Arthur Clennam, son of the woman for whom she
works, who is convinced that his mother has, in some way,
wronged Little Dorrit or the Dorrit family. Straightening this

out so that the good people may get their just rewards and
the bad people be punished is the main theme of the novel,
although, as in all Dickens' works, there are several subthemes
that wander far afield. Through the efforts initiated by Arthur a hidden fortune is unearthed for Mr. Dorrit and he goes
grandly to Italy with his two daughters, although Little Dorrit never takes a place in the social whirl that surrounds
them. Arthur's business fails and he is confined to the Marshalsea in the same room that Mr. Dorrit had occupied. When
he falls ill, Little Dorrit comes to the prison, in her old prison
dress, to care for him. She offers to lend him money to pay
his debts, but the noble youth spurns such a solution to his
problem. Then the Dorrits lose all their money, Mr. Dorrit
dies, Arthur's partner returns and straightens out their affairs,
and Arthur and Little Dorrit go from the prison to the church
to be married.

Another saintly maiden who is held in thrall by her self-
sacrificing sense of duty to her father is Madeline Bray in
Nicholas Nickleby. Madeline's father is a much more reprehensible character than Little Dorrit's. The latter is only
weak and silly; the former is totally evil and thoroughly con-
scienceless. But Madeline devoted her life to his interests and
is willing to give herself to a horrible old man for his benefit.

Nicholas first sees Madeline in an employment office where
he has gone to seek a position as a tutor. She is seventeen at
the time, "of very slight and delicate figure, but exquisitely
shaped, who, walking timidly up to the desk, made an inquiry, in a very low tone of voice, relative to some situation
as governess, or companion to a lady. She raised her veil, for
an instant, while she preferred the inquiry, and disclosed a
countentance of most uncommon beauty, though shaded by

a cloud of sadness, which in one so young was doubly remarkable."

Nineteen-year-old Nicholas cannot forget the beautiful, sad face, which he again encounters in the parlor of the twin Cheeryble brothers, affluent businessmen who have befriended and employed him. Entering the room with a letter, Nicholas sees the girl kneeling at the feet of brother Charles. As the older man raises her she swoons and Nicholas is sent from the room. He still does not know who she is, but this is soon remedied when the brothers give him a secret and delicate commission involving the girl and tell him her story.

Many years before, Charles Cheeryble had loved the girl's mother, but she had married another, who had mistreated her badly. "The mother was a gentle, loving, confiding creature, and although he wounded her from their marriage until her death as cruelly and wantonly as ever man did, she never ceased to love him. She commended him on her deathbed to her child's care. Her child has never forgotten it, and never will."

Madeline spurns all offers of aid from her mother's friends, and from her grandfather, which are conditional on her leaving her worthless father. He is now, sick and poverty stricken, living within "the Rules" of King's Bench Prison, which means that he is a debtor who has paid a fee to live outside the prison walls but still be free from further persecution by his creditors. Charles would gladly relieve the girl of all her financial burdens, but she will take only a pittance. For this she comes secretly, by night, knowing that if her father knew of such an easy source of money he would squander it. Now the brothers have a plan to help Madeline openly. She is an accomplished painter and they send Nicholas, who is unknown to her and her father, to give her art commissions. They do not know that Nicholas is already half in love with her, although he has never spoken to the girl.

Nicholas calls upon the Brays and meets the querulous and imperious father, whose features "presented the remains of a handsome countenance, but one in which the embers of strong and impetuous passions were easier to be traced than any expression which would have rendered a far plainer face much more prepossessing." When he leaves a five-pound note as a deposit, the father orders Madeline to summon a servant girl. "Tell her to get it changed, to get me a newspaper, to buy me some grapes, another bottle of the wine that I had last week —and—and—I forget half I want just now, but she can go out again. Let her get those first, those first. Now, Madeline, my love, quick, quick! Good God, how slow you are!"

" 'He remembers nothing that *she* wants,' thought Nicholas."

Meanwhile, a senile and slimy moneylender, Arthur Gride, is conspiring with Nicholas' nefarious uncle Ralph, the major villain of the piece, to get Madeline as his bride. Gride is "a little old man, of about seventy or seventy-five years of age, of a very lean figure, much bent, and slightly twisted. . . . His nose and chin were sharp and prominent, his jaws had fallen inwards from loss of teeth, his face was shrivelled and yellow, save where the cheeks were streaked with the colour of a dry winter apple; and where his beard had been, there lingered yet a few grey tufts which seemed, like the ragged eyebrows, to denote the badness of the soil from which they sprung. The whole air and attitude of the form was one of stealthy cat-like obsequiousness; the whole expression of the face was concentrated in a wrinkled leer, compounded of cunning, lecherousness, slyness, and avarice."

This old lecher tells Ralph Nickleby that he plans to marry.

" 'To some old hag?' asks Ralph. 'No,' says Gride, 'to a young and beautiful girl; fresh, lovely, bewitching, and not nineteen. Dark eyes, long eyelashes, ripe and ruddy lips that to look at is to long to kiss, beautiful clustering hair that one's fingers itch to play with, such a waist as might make a man clasp the air involuntarily thinking of twining his arm about it, little feet that tread so lightly they hardly seem to walk upon the ground—to marry all this, sir, this—hey, hey!' "

Gride's scheme is simple, taking into consideration the character of Madeline's father. Ralph and he are the man's only debtors. The moneylender proposes to offer a discharge of his debts and an allowance to live well in France as the price for his daughter. Gride knows that Bray could not resist such an offer. "And if he could not resist *me*, do you think his daughter could resist *him?* Shouldn't I have her Mrs. Arthur Gride—pretty Mrs. Arthur Gride—a tit-bit—a dainty chick—shouldn't I have her Mrs. Arthur Gride in a week, a month, a day—any time I chose to name?" Gride also knows that he is making a profitable investment, for he has secret knowledge that Madeline will inherit a legacy from her maternal grandfather when she marries or comes of age. The old man offers to pay Ralph, a more capable negotiator, five hundred pounds to make the deal.

The two call on Bray, who falls in with their evil scheme without much effort. While they are there Madeline enters and the father has a relapse. "It might have moved a very hard and wordly heart to see the young and beautiful creature, whose certain misery they had been contriving but a minute before, throw her arms about her father's neck, and pour forth words of tender sympathy and love, the sweetest a father's ear can know, or child's lips form. But Ralph looked coldly on; and Arthur Gride, whose bleared eyes gloated only over the outward beauties, and were blind to the spirit which reigned within, evinced—a fantastic kind of warmth certainly, but not exactly that kind of warmth of feeling which the contemplation of virtue usually inspires."

Nicholas learns of the impending marriage only on the day before it is to take place. The Cheeryble brothers are out of town and the distraught young man calls on Madeline to plead with her, as their representative, to postpone this evil event. He tells her: " 'You are betrayed, and sold for money: for gold, whose every coin is rusted with tears, if not red with the blood of ruined men, who have fallen desperately by their own mad hands.'

" 'You say you have a duty to discharge,' said Madeline, 'and so have I. And with the help of Heaven I will perform mine.'

" 'Say rather with the help of devils,' replied Nicholas; 'with the help of men, one of them your destined husband, who are ——.'

" 'I must not hear this,' cried the young lady, striving to repress a shudder, occasioned, as it seemed, even by this slight allusion to Arthur Gride. 'This evil, if evil it be, has been of my own seeking. I am impelled to this course by no one, but follow it of my own free will. You see I am not constrained or forced. Report this,' said Madeline, 'to my dear friend and benefactor, and, taking with you my prayers and thanks for him and for yourself, leave me for ever!' "

The wedding day dawns. Ralph Nickleby and Gride are waiting downstairs in the Bray home for the father to bring Madeline down. The door flies open and Nicholas enters, accompanied by his sister Kate, a girl of Madeline's age. He has come to take the girl by force is necessary to prevent the nuptials. As he defies the two scoundrels there is a thud upstairs followed by a succession of screams. Those below rush up to find Bray dead on the floor with Madeline swooning over his body. Nicholas sweeps her up and, followed by Kate, takes her to the home of their mother. Here she is nursed by Kate through a long illness, during which the sister sings the praises of the brother to the point that Madeline realizes that she loves him. By this time it has become known that Madeline will inherit twelve thousand pounds when she marries and honor prohibits Nicholas, who has only his meager salary from the Cheeryble brothers, from proclaiming his love. But the brothers tell him that this is nonsense; that Madeline loves him and that he will surely manage her money well. They virtually throw him into the girl's arms and the young couple wed.

Florence Dombey has both a brother and a father for whom to sacrifice herself. The latter first ignores her, then rejects her, then disdains her, and finally, in the closing pages of the novel, comes to realize that his attitude toward her has been the great and cruel mistake of his life. Her brother Paul clings to her throughout his short life in lieu of his mother who dies at his birth and his father who is obsessed with the pursuit of money and power and who has no natural feeling of affection for his children.

Mr. Dombey is the prototype of what modern behavioral scientists term a rejective parent; in Florence's case consciously, in Paul's unconsciously. He professes to love Paul deeply, but as a child he rejects him, and, as a result, destroys him. He sees Paul not as a child, but as the son of Dombey and Son. Childhood is something to get over as quickly as possible so that Paul may take his place in the business which is Mr. Dombey's universe. "The earth was made for Dombey and Son to trade in, and the sun and moon to

give them light. . . . rainbows gave them promise of fair
weather; winds blew for or against their enterprises; stars
and planets circled in their orbits, to preserve inviolate a system of which they were the center." Therefore Dombey and
Son must have a male heir.

Mr. Dombey is beside himself with joy when Paul is born.
Six years earlier the Dombeys had had a daughter, Florence,
but this child is of no interest to Mr. Dombey; he scarcely
knows her. "His feeling about the child had been negative
from her birth. He had never conceived an aversion to her:
it had not been worth his while or in his humour. She had
never been a positively disagreeable object to him. But now
he was ill at ease about her. She troubled his peace. He would
have preferred to put her idea aside altogether, if he had
known how. Perhaps—who shall decide on such mysteries!—
he was afraid that he might come to hate her."

Florence is introduced into the story at Paul's birth, when
her father tells her: "Florence, you may go and look at your
pretty brother, if you like, I dare say. Don't touch him!" Instead, Florence runs to the bed and throws her arms around
her mother. She is still clinging to her when the mother dies.
A few days later the relationship between father and daughter is further established by a conversation between Paul's
nurse, Polly Richards, and Susan Nipper, a fourteen-year-old
servant girl who has Florence in her care. The child had been
sent away for the funeral.

" 'She'll be quite happy, now she has come home again,'
said Polly, nodding to her with an encouraging smile upon
her wholesome face, 'and will be so pleased to see her dear
papa to-night.'

" 'Lork, Mrs. Richards!' cried Miss Nipper, taking up her

words with a jerk. 'Don't. See her dear papa indeed! I should like to see her do it!'

" 'Won't she then?' asked Polly.

" 'Lork, Mrs. Richards, no, her pa's a deal too wrapped up in somebody else, and before there was somebody else to be wrapped up in she never was a favourite; girls are thrown away in this house, Mrs. Richards, *I* assure.' "

The nurse looks sorrowfully after Florence as she leaves the room. "The child in her grief and neglect was so gentle, so quiet, and uncomplaining, was possessed of so much affection that no one seemed to care to have, and so much sorrowful intelligence that no one seemed to mind or think about the wounding of, that Polly's heart was sore when she was left alone again."

Florence tries to go to her father. "When little Florence timidly presented herself, Mr. Dombey stopped in his pacing up and down and looked towards her. Had he looked with greater interest and with a father's eye, he might have read in her keen glance the impulses and fears that made her waver —the passionate desire to run clinging to him, crying, as she hid her face in his embrace, 'Oh, father, try to love me! there's no one else'; the dread of repulse; the fear of being too bold, and of offending him; the pitiable need in which she stood of some assurance and encouragement, and how her overcharged young heart was wandering to find some natural resting-place, for its sorrow and affection.

"But he saw nothing of this. He saw her pause irresolutely at the door and look towards him; and he saw no more."

The story jumps forward five years. Paul, at this age, "was a pretty little fellow, though there was something wan and wistful in his small face. . . . He was childish and sportive enough at times, and not of a sullen disposition; but he had a strange, old-fashioned, thoughtful way, at other times, of sitting brooding in his miniature arm-chair, when he looked (and talked) like one of those terrible little beings in the fairy tales, who, at a hundred and fifty or two hundred years of age, fantastically represent the children for whom they have been substituted. He would frequently be stricken with this precocious mood upstairs in the nursery; and would sometimes lapse into it suddenly, exclaiming that he was tired, even while playing with Florence."

The child is sickly and never at ease except in the company of his eleven-year-old sister, who devotes herself to his care. But his father requires that they have an evening session of sitting together by the fire and talking, man to man. The child's introspective periods are most frequent when he is with his father. One conversation is an interesting exploration, by Dickens, into a child's understanding of the adult world.

"On one of these occasions, when they had both been perfectly quiet for a long time, and Mr. Dombey only knew that the child was awake by occasionally glancing at his eye, where the bright fire was sparkling like a jewel, little Paul broke silence thus:

" 'Papa! what's money?'

"The abrupt question had such immediate reference to the subject of Mr. Dombey's thoughts that Mr. Dombey was quite disconcerted.

" 'What is money, Paul?' he answered. 'Money?'

" 'Yes,' said the child, laying his hands upon the elbows of his little chair, and turning the old face up towards Mr. Dombey's, 'what is money?'

"Mr. Dombey was in a difficulty. He would have liked to give him some explanation involving the terms circulating-medium currency, depreciation of currency, paper, bullion, rates of exchange, value of precious metals in the market, and so forth; but looking down at the little chair, and seeing what a long way down it was, he answered: 'Gold, and silver, and copper. Guineas, shillings, half-pence. You know what they are?'

" 'Oh yes, I know what they are,' said Paul. 'I don't mean that, papa. I mean what's money after all.'

"Heaven and earth! how old his face was as he turned it up again towards his father's!

" 'What is money after all?' said Mr. Dombey, backing his chair a little, that he might the better gaze in sheer amaze-ment at the presumptuous atom that propounded such an inquiry.

" 'I mean, papa, what can it do?' returned Paul, folding his arms (they were hardly long enough to fold), and looking at the fire, and up at him, and at the fire, and up at him again.

"Mr. Dombey drew his chair back to its former place, and patted him on the head. 'You'll know better by and by, my man,' he said. 'Money, Paul, can do anything.' He took hold of the little hand, and beat it softly against one of his own, as he said so.

"But Paul got his hand free as soon as he could; and rub-bing it gently to and fro on the elbow of his chair, as if his wit were in the palm, and he were sharpening it—and looking at the fire again, as though the fire had been his adviser and prompter—repeated, after a short pause:

" 'Anything, papa?'

" 'Yes. Anything—almost,' said Mr. Dombey.

" 'Anything means everything, don't it, papa?' asked his son, not observing, or possibly not understanding, the quali-fication.

" 'It includes it: yes,' said Mr. Dombey.

" 'Why didn't money save me my mamma?' returned the child. 'It isn't cruel, is it?'

" 'Cruel!' said Mr. Dombey, settling his neckcloth, and seeming to resent the idea. 'No. A good thing can't be cruel.'

" 'If it's a good thing, and can do anything,' said the little fellow, thoughtfully, as he looked back at the fire, 'I wonder why it didn't save me my mamma.' "

At the age of five Paul is sent to Mrs. Pipchin's Infantile Boarding Establishment by the sea for his health. Florence, of course, goes along to care for him. He spends much of his time in a carriage on the beach, watching the waves. He does not want to play with other children. When one approaches to ask how he feels, " 'I am very well, I thank you,' he would answer. 'But you had better go and play, if you please.'

"Then he would turn his head, and watch the child go away, and say to Florence: 'We don't want any others, do we? Kiss me, Floy.' "

Next year Paul is sent to Mr. Blimber's boarding school to be crammed with education so that he may sooner take his rightful place in Dombey and Son. Florence stays nearby with Susan so that she may be with him on weekends. Paul is floundering in the school until Florence has Susan buy duplicate books so that she can tutor him on Saturdays. But the strain is too much for the weak boy; by the time he is seven he is back home, confined to his bed, with his sister as his constant companion. Despite a cordon of doctors Paul slowly declines. As the end nears he has visions of a river that will carry him to a mysterious beyond. In his last hour he says: " 'Now lay me down and Floy, come close to me, and let me see you!'

"Sister and brother wound their arms around each other,

and the golden light came streaming in, and fell upon them, locked together.

" 'How fast the river runs, between its green banks and the rushes, Floy! But it's very near the sea. I hear the waves! They always said so!'

"Presently he told her that the motion of the boat upon the stream was lulling him to rest. How green the banks were now, how bright the flowers growing on them, and how tall the rushes! Now the boat was out at sea, but gliding smoothly on. And now there was a shore before him. Who stood on the bank!

"He put his hands together, as he had been used to do at his prayers. He did not remove his arms to do it; but they saw him fold them so, behind her neck.

" 'Mamma is like you, Floy. I know her by the face! But tell them that the print upon the stairs at school is not divine enough. The light about the head is shining on me as I go!'

"The golden ripple on the wall came back again, and nothing else stirred in the room. The old, old fashion! The fashion that came in with our first garments, and will last unchanged until our race has run its course, and the wide firmament is rolled up like a scroll. The old, old fashion—Death!"

Florence's one great wish after her brother's death is to be able to console her father; to express to him the great love and tenderness that she feels. Every night after the house is still she goes to her father's room and "crouched upon the cold stone floor outside it . . . to listen even for his breath; and in her one absorbing wish to be allowed to show him some affection." On one occasion when she gathers her courage to go into his room and speak to him at night the father assumes that the child is frightened and leads her to the foot of the stairs that ascend to her room.

Dombey goes away shortly after the funeral, leaving Florence alone in the house with Susan and the other servants. The child lives with her books, her teachers, and her music and with her dedication to her love for her father. She could go into his room now, and made a daily pilgrimage there. "She could look upon the objects that had surrounded him in his sorrow, and could nestle near his chair, and not dread the glance that she so well remembered. She could render him such little tokens of her duty and service, as putting everything in order for him with her own hands, binding little nosegays for his table, changing them as one by one they withered, and he did not come back, preparing something for him every day, and leaving some timid mark of her presence near his usual seat. To-day, it was a little painted stand for his watch; to-morrow she would be afraid to leave it, and would substitute some other trifle of her making not so likely to attract his eye. Waking in the night, perhaps, she would tremble at the thought of his coming home and angrily rejecting it, and would hurry down with slippered feet and quickly beating heart, and bring it away. At another time, she would only lay her face upon his desk, and leave a kiss there, and a tear."

When Florence is in her mid-teens her father buys himself a beautiful young wife, Edith—or Edith's mother fosters the match because of the older man's wealth and position. Edith and Florence quickly become very close, more like younger and older sisters than stepmother and stepdaughter. But the marriage does not go well. Edith is conscious that she has been traded by her scheming mother and is too proud to bend before her demanding husband. On the second anniversary of their marriage she leaves him. Dombey by this time time has developed a strange feeling toward his daughter akin to hatred. He associates her with the loss of his son and his wife. Now he orders her from the house.

Florence goes to the home of an old sea captain whom she has long known, outside the family. The captain has also befriended a young man named Malter Gay, a clerk at Dombey and Son whom Florence has loved since she was twelve and who loves her. Malter was sent some years before to the Barbadoes and his ship was lost at sea. Now he suddenly returns and he and Florence are soon married. But this does not change her dedication toward her father. Despite the fact that he sent her away, she feels that she has deserted him.

A year passes—Florence is now in her late teens—and the house of Dombey and Son fails. The father pays off its debts, leaving himself virtually penniless. His large house is to be sold and the movers are carting away the furniture as he crouches in his room. Finally, he comes to realize the wrong that he has done Florence. "He knew now, what it was to be rejected and deserted; now, when every loving blossom he had withered in his innocent daughter's heart was snowing down in ashes on him.

"He thought of her, as she had been that night when he and his bride came home. He thought of her as she had been, in all the home-events of the abandoned house. He thought, now, that of all around him, she alone had never changed. His boy had faded into dust, his proud wife had sunk into a polluted creature, his flatterer and friend had been transformed into the worst of villains, his riches had melted away, the very walls that sheltered him looked on him as a stranger; she alone had turned the same mild gentle look upon him always. Yes, to the latest and the last. She had never changed to him—nor had he ever changed to her—and she was lost."

But of course Florence is not lost. As the old man reaches the depth of his despondency he hears a cry: " 'Papa! Dearest papa! Pardon me, forgive me! I have come back to ask forgiveness on my knees. I never can be happy more, without it!'

"Unchanged still. Of all the world, unchanged. Raising the same face to his, as on that miserable night. Asking *his* forgiveness! ...

"He tottered to his chair. He felt her draw his arms about her neck; he felt her put her own round his; he felt her kisses on his face; he felt her wet cheek laid against his own; he felt —oh, how deeply!—all that he had done.

"Upon the breast that he had bruised, against the heart that he had almost broken, she laid his face, now covered with his hands."

So Florence's years of selfless devotion are rewarded. Her father collapses and is nursed by Florence and then comes to live with his daughter, her husband, and the two children that soon appear. He basks in his daughter's love and in his own finally kindled feeling for his child. "Autumn days are shining, and on the sea-beach there are often a young lady, and a white-haired gentleman. With them, or near them, are two children; boy and girl. . . . The white-haired gentleman walks with the little boy . . . helps him in his play. Sometimes when the child is sitting by his side and looks up in his face, asking him questions, he takes the tiny hand in his, and holding it, forgets to answer. Then the child says: " 'What, Grandpapa, am I so like my poor little uncle again?'

" 'Yes, Paul; but he was weak and you are very strong.'

" 'Oh, yes, I am very strong.'

" 'And he lay on a little bed beside the sea, and you can run about.' And so they range away again busily, for the white-haired gentleman likes best to see the child free and stirring."

CHAPTER

V

~

CHILDREN AT SCHOOL

Dickens sent his fictional children to some thirty schools— most of them bad schools. Education was one of his long- term targets as a reformer, and his pen limned a wide variety of institutions that typified the inadequacies of English edu- cation—schools ranging from the merely ludicrous to the downright vicious. Some Dickensians have labeled him the most effective spokesman for educational reform in his era. Wrote one contemporary: "He should be immortalized if only for his putting down school tyrannies, exposing and crushing school pretentions, and doubtless saving many a fair intellect from withering blight and perversion."

The novelist was concerned with schools as such, with schoolmasters and teachers, and with curriculum and methods. But he was more concerned with the over-all neglect of edu- cation for the mass of children that characterized English society of his day. And he was particularly disturbed at the terrible injustice of punishing the children of the poor for

126

something for which they were not responsible—ignorance. In the preface to *Nicholas Nickleby* he cited the existence of the Yorkshire schools as an example of "the monstrous neglect of education in England and the disregard of it by the state as a means of forming good and bad citizens."

In *Household Words* he wrote: "I saw a Minister of State, sitting in his Closet; and all around him, rising from the country that he governed, up to the Eternal Heavens, was a low dull howl of ignorance. It was a wild inexplicable mutter, confused but full of threatening, and it made all hearers' hearts quake within them. But, few heard. In the single city where this Minister of State was seated, I saw Thirty Thousand children hunted, flogged, imprisoned, but not taught—who might have been nurtured by the wolf or the bear, so little of humanity had they within them or without."

In another essay he wrote: " 'And in my history for the Month of May,' said the Old Year of 1852 with a groan, 'I find it written: Two little children whose heads scarcely reached the top of the desk were charged at Bow Street on the seventh, with stealing a loaf out of a baker's shop. They said in defence that they were starving, and their appearance showed that they spoke the truth. They were sentenced to be whipped in the House of Correction.' To be whipped! Woe, Woe! can the State devise no better sentence for its little children? *Will it never sentence them to be taught?*"

In his novels Dickens sometimes digressed to introduce characters or situations to point up the horrors of ignorance and to castigate the official lack of interest in widespread education. In *Old Curiosity Shop*, when Little Nell goes into a poor home to ask for food, she observes this scene—a vignette which has nothing to do with the story line and is created solely to advance the author's crusade:

"It seemed that a couple of poor families lived in this hovel, for two women, each among children of her own, occupied different portions of the room. In the centre stood a grave gentleman in black who appeared to have just entered, and who held by the arm a boy.

" 'Here, woman,' he said, 'here's your deaf and dumb son. You may thank me for restoring him to you. He was brought before me, this morning, charged with theft; and with any other boy it would have gone hard, I assure you. But, as I had compassion on his infirmities, and thought he might have learnt no better, I have managed to bring him back to you. Take more care of him for the future.'

" 'And won't you give me back *my* son!' said the other woman, hastily rising and confronting him. 'Won't you give me back *my* son, sir, who was transported for the same offence!'

" 'Was *he* deaf and dumb, woman?' asked the gentleman sternly.

" 'Was he not, sir?'

" 'You know he was not.'

" 'He was,' cried the woman. 'He was deaf, dumb, and blind to all that was good and right, from his cradle. Her boy may have learnt no better! Where did mine learn better? where could he? who was there to teach him better, or where was it to be learnt?'

" 'Peace, woman,' said the gentleman, 'your boy was in possession of all his senses.'

" 'He was,' cried the mother; 'and he was the more easy to be led astray because he had them. If you save this boy because he may not know right from wrong, why did you not save mine who was never taught the difference? You gentlemen have as good a right to punish her boy, that God has kept in ignorance of sound and speech, as you have to punish mine, that you kept in ignorance yourselves. How many of the girls and boys—ah, men and women too—that are brought before you, and you don't pity, are deaf and dumb in their minds, and go wrong in that state, and are punished in that state, body and soul, while you gentlemen are quarrelling among yourselves whether they ought to learn this or that?— Be a just man, sir, and give me back my son.' "

Dickens' deep interest in schooling and education undoubtedly stemmed from his own experience in this area; to the end of his life he frequently bemoaned his lack of a formal education. Two schools that he did attend briefly he later caricatured in novels. When he was six he went to a dame school with his sister Fanny, conduced by "a grim and unsympathetic old personage, flavoured with musty dry lavender and dressed in black crepe," who, in his mind, "ruled the world with a birch." This old lady later became Mrs. Pipchin, the owner of the Infantile Boarding Establishment to which Paul Dombey was sent, "a marvelous, ill-favoured, ill-conditioned old lady, of a stooping figure, with a mottled face like bad marble, a hook nose, and a hard grey eye, that looked as if it might have been hammered at on an anvil without sustaining any injury. . . .

"She was held to be an old lady of remarkable firmness, who was quite scientific in the knowledge of the childish character—it being a part of Mrs. Pipchin's system not to encourage a child's mind to develop and expand itself like a young flower, but to open it by force like an oyster, the moral of [her Early Readings] was usually of a violent and stunning character—the hero (a naughty boy) seldom, in the mildest catastrophe, being finished off by anything less than a lion or a bear. Such was life at Mrs. Pipchin's."

In a letter to a friend at the time when this passage appeared in an early installment of *Dombey and Son*, the author wrote: "I hope you will like Mrs. Pipchin's establishment. It is from life and I was there—I don't suppose I was eight years old; but I remember it as well, and certainly understood it as well, as I do now."

The second school that Dickens attended, Wellington House Academy, was immortalized as Salem Hill in *David Copperfield*, and its proprietor, William Jones, became Mr. Creakle. One of Dickens' schoolmates later said that David Copperfield's description of the schoolroom at Salem Hall was an accurate description of the actual room where he and Charles had gone to school.

"I see it now. A long room, with three long rows of desks, and six of forms, and bristling all round with pegs for hats and slates. Scraps of old copy-books and exercises litter the dirty floor. Some silkworms' houses, made of the same materials, are scattered over the desks. Two miserable little white mice, left behind by their owner, are running up and down in a fusty castle made of pasteboard and wire, looking in all the corners with their red eyes for anything to eat. A bird, in a cage very little bigger than himself, makes a mournful rattle now and then in hopping on his perch, two inches high, or dropping from it, but neither sings nor chirps. There is a strange unwholesome smell upon the room, like mildewed corduroys, sweet apples wanting air, and rotten books. There could not well be more ink splashed about it, if it had been roofless from its first construction, and the skies had rained, snowed, hailed, and blown ink through the varying seasons of the year."

In a speech late in life Dickens harked back to the type of institution represented by Wellington House-Salem Hall and said: "I don't like the sort of school to which I once went myself, the respected proprietor of which was by far the most ignorant man I have ever had the pleasure to know, who was one of the worst-tempered men perhaps that ever lived, whose business it was to make as much out of us and to put as little into us as possible. . . .

"I don't like that sort of school, because I don't see what business the master had to be at the top of it instead of the bottom, and because I never could understand the wholesomeness of the moral preached by the abject appearance and degraded condition of the teachers. . . .

"I do not like that sort of school, because I have never yet lost my ancient suspicion touching that curious coincidence that the boy with four brothers to come always got the prizes. In fact, and in short, I do not like that sort of school, which is a pernicious and abominable humbug altogether."

Although Dickens in later life seriously averred that he did not like the type of school represented by Wellington House, some of his autobiographical writings seem to indicate that he was not too unhappy there. He was a day student and the beatings that he described so graphically in fiction were, in fact, usually limited to boarders, who could not carry their woes home to parents at night. Dickens wrote amusingly and with seeming affection of some of the anecdotes and personalities that were part of his brief school days, characteristically exaggerating and embroidering them. Thus, in "Birthday Celebration," he recalled the change in the demeanor of the school bully when that worthy learned that Charles might soon receive a package containing guava jelly from the West Indies:

"I had mentioned these hints in confidence to a few friends, and had promised to give away, as I now see reason to believe, a handsome covey of partridges potted, and about a hundredweight of guava jelly. It was now that Globson, bully no more, sought me out on the playground. He was a big fat boy, with a big fat head and a big fat fist, and at the beginning of that Half had raised such a bump on my forehead that I couldn't get my hat of state on, to go to Church. He said that after an interval of reflection (four months) he now felt this blow to have been an error of judgment, and that he wished to apologize for the same.

"Not only that but holding down his big head between his two big hands in order that I might reach it conveniently, he requested me, as an act of justice which would appease his awakened conscience, to raise a retributive bump upon it, in the presence of witnesses.

"This handsome proposal I modestly declined, and he then embraced me, and we walked away conversing. We conversed respecting the West India Islands, and in the pursuit of knowledge he asked me with much interest whether in the course of my reading I had met with any reliable description of the mode of manufacturing guava jelly; or whether I had ever happened to taste that conserve, which he had been given to understand was of rare excellence."

Many of Dickens' novels attacked the unqualified teachers who were commonplace of the day. (In one town a man was appointed schoolmaster when age made him incompetent to take care of the pigs.) A schoolmaster in a charity school in *Dombey and Son* was a superannuated old man "of savage disposition, who had been appointed schoolmaster because he didn't know anything, and wasn't fit for anything, and for whose cruel cane all chubby little boys had a perfect fascination." David Copperfield's master, Creakle, was "an incapable brute, who had no more right to be possessed of the great trust he held, than to be Lord High Admiral, or Commander-in-Chief." In the first of the Boz sketches, titled "Our Parish," Dickens did a thumbnail sketch of the pauper schoolmaster, an individual "on whom misfortune seems to have set her mark; nothing he ever did or was concerned in appears to have prospered." When all else had failed he had applied to the parish for relief, and "some kind-hearted man who had known him in happier times chanced to be church warden that year, and through his interest, he was appointed to his present situation."

Dame schools were worse, if possible, than those run by men. No degree of competence was expected from female teachers. The list of qualifications for mistresses in the old charity schools specifically excluded "that part which relates to writing a good hand, and understanding of Arithmetic." Dickens' finest portrayal of an incompetent teacher is his humorous description of the school run by Mr. Wopsle's great-aunt in *Great Expectations:*

"Mr. Wopsle's great-aunt kept an evening-school in the village; that is to say, she was a ridiculous old woman of limited means and unlimited infirmity, who used to go to sleep from six to seven every evening, in the society of youth who paid twopence per week each, for the improving opportunity of seeing her do it. . . .

"The educational Scheme or Course established by Mr. Wopsle's great-aunt may be resolved into the following synopsis. The pupils ate apples and put straws down one another's backs, until Mr. Wopsle's great-aunt collected her energies and made an indiscriminate totter at them with a birch-rod. After receiving the charge with every mark of derision, the pupils formed in line and buzzingly passed a ragged book from hand to hand. The book had an alphabet in it, some figures and tables, and a little spelling—that is to say, it had had once. As soon as this volume began to circulate, Mr. Wopsle's great-aunt fell into a state of coma, arising either from sleep or a rheumatic paroxysm. The pupils then entered among themselves upon a competitive examination on the subject of Boots, with the view of ascertaining who could tread the hardest upon whose toes. This mental exercise lasted until Biddy made a rush at them and distributed three defaced Bibles (shaped as if they had been unskillfully cut off the chump-end of something), more illegibly printed at the best than any curiosities of literature I have since met with, speckled all over with iron mould, and having various specimens of the insect world smashed between their leaves. This part of the Course was usually lightened by several single combats between Biddy and refractory students. When the fights were over, Biddy gave out the number of a page, and then we all read aloud what we could—or what we couldn't—in a frightful chorus, Biddy leading with a high, shrill, monotonous voice, and none of us having the least notion of, or reverence for, what we were reading about. When this horrible din had lasted a certain time, it mechanically awoke Mr. Wopsle's great-aunt, who staggered at a boy fortuitously, and pulled his ears. This was understood to terminate the course for the evening and we emerged into the air with shrieks of intellectual victory."

Dickens' interest in schools extended beyond his writing. Several of his lecture-readings were benefits for educational institutions. He visited upwards of seventy schools in England, Europe, and America, in addition to the twelve to which, at one time or another, he sent his own children. At the request of the Baroness Burdett-Coutts, who was considering them as a philanthropy, he investigated the Ragged

Schools. These were voluntary institutions for poor children, the first of which had been started by a shoemaker and a chimney sweep. Dickens was deeply moved by his visit to one such school that was located among the scenes that he had described so graphically in *Oliver Twist*. The school, he wrote, was an "awful sight." It was "held in three most wretched rooms on the first floor of a rotten house; every plank, and timber, and brick, and lath, and piece of plastering of which shakes as you walk. One room is devoted to the girls; two to the boys. The former are better looking—I cannot say better dressed, for there is no such thing as dress among the seventy pupils; certainly not the elements of a whole suit of clothes, among them all. I have seldom seen, in all the strange and dreadful things I have seen in London and elsewhere, anything so shocking as the dire neglect of soul and body exhibited among these children. And although I know, and am as sure as it is possible for one to be of anything which has not happened, that in the prodigious misery and ignorance of the swarming masses of mankind in England, the seeds of its certain ruin are sown; I never saw that Truth so staring out in hopeless characters, as it does from the walls of this place. The children in the Jails are almost as common sights to me as my own; but these are worse, for they have not yet arrived there, but are as plainly and as certainly traveling there, as they are to their graves."

Dickens recommended that Miss Coutts support the Ragged Schools at that time, and he was a valuable ally of these schools in their early years, although he had strong reservations about certain aspects of them, particularly the emphasis placed on religion and the lack of qualifications of the Masters who were volunteers without special training as teachers. "The teachers in those schools," he wrote, "though devoted

to their uninviting work, are so narrow minded and odd—
and the whole thing (which might be so good) is such a
scramble." Of one of the teachers he said: "She seems to me
to be always blowing a shrill set of spiritual Pan's pipes—but
she is earnest, though bitterly in want of sound teaching for
the office of teacher." The only portrayal of a Ragged School
in a novel—the one that Charley Hexam attended in *Our
Mutual Friend*—was a satirical one in which the teachers,
"animated solely by good intentions, had no idea of execution, and a lamentable jumble was the upshot of their kind
endeavours."

The first school that Dickens described in print was a
prison institution in the Boz sketch "A Visit to Newgate."
"We were led through a narrow yard to the 'school'—a portion of the prison set apart for boys under fourteen years of
age. In a tolerable-sized room, in which were writing materials and some copy-books, was the schoolmaster with a
couple of his pupils; the remainder having been fetched from
an adjoining apartment, the whole were drawn up for our
inspection. There were fourteen of them in all, some with
shoes, some without, some in pinafores without jackets, others
in jackets without pinafores, and one in scarce anything at
all. The whole number, without an exception, we believe,
had been committed for trial on charges of pocket-picking;
and fourteen such terrible little faces we never beheld—there
was not one redeeming feature among them—not a glance of
honesty—not a wink expressive of anything except the gallows
and the hulks, in the whole collection. As to anything like
shame or contrition, that was entirely out of the question.
They were evidently quite gratified at being thought worth
the trouble of looking at; their idea seemed to be that we
had come to see Newgate as a grand affair, and they were an

indispensable part of the show; and every boy, as he 'fell in' to the line, actually seemed as pleased and important as if he had done something excessively meritorious in getting there at all. We never looked upon a more disagreeable sight, because we never saw fourteen such hopeless creatures of neglect before."

Dickens' most famous piece of educational crusading, and some of his most graphic descriptive writing on the hardships of neglected children, was the first portion of the novel *Nicholas Nickleby*, which exposed a group of schools that flourished principally in the County of Yorkshire. As these were presented by Dickens through the fictional prototype Dotheboys Hall, they were schools for unwanted children whose parents or other adults could pay a pittance to get rid of them. Their principal merit from the standpoint of those responsible for the children was that they were cheap and kept the youngsters year round; there were no vacations. In many cases neither parents nor schools seemed to be much concerned as to what, if anything, the children learned, how they were fed, dressed, treated, or mistreated.

Dickens' first interest in the Yorkshire schools came, he said, from a tale he heard of "a suppurated abscess that some boy had come home with, in consequence of his Yorkshire guide, philosopher, and friend having ripped it open with an inky penknife. The impression made upon me, however made, never left me." There was other evidence of the horrors of these institutions. In a lawsuit in 1823 a boy testified: "I felt a weakness in my eyes, and could not write my copy; Mr. Shaw said that he would beat me; and on the following day I could not see at all, and I told Mr. Shaw, who sent me and three others to the washhouse. I staid in the washhouse about a month . . . there were nine boys totally blind."

In preparation for writing *Nicholas Nickleby*, Dickens, accompanied by his illustrator, Browne, made a visit to Yorkshire to investigate some schools. On his trip he visited a graveyard and saw, "on that dreary afternoon," the graves of twenty-four boys between seven and eighteen who had died at a single academy. The first gravestone he stumbled on "was placed above the grave of a boy, eighteen long years old . . . I suppose his heart broke . . . I think his ghost put poor Smike in my mind, upon the spot."

The writer, using a fictitious name, carried a letter of introduction representing him as a friend of a recent widow who was looking for an inexpensive school for her boy. In the preface to the several editions to the book, Dickens reiterated that both Dotheboys Hall and its headmaster, Squeers, were not based on any specific institution or individual, but that they were typical of the area; in fact, he claimed that he had toned down the horrors that actually existed because the bare truth would be considered too exaggerated if presented as fiction. Yet he was delighted when he learned that some Yorkshire masters were planning to take action against him for libel, presumably seeing themselves in the villainous Squeers. Controversy raged for years as to whether the conditions Dickens portrayed represented a true picture of the schools as a class, but there is general agreement that the book did much to curtail if not eradicate them.

Nicholas Nickleby starts with the death of the improvident father of its nineteen-year-old hero, leaving the boy, his mother, and his seventeen-year-old sister Kate penniless. Kate is a raven-haired beauty innocent in the ways of the world. Mrs. Nickleby is a rather foolish, verbose, pretentious character prone to dilate on her fancied better days and connections: a caricature of the author's mother, "who had at no time been remarkable for the possession of a very clear understanding," and who has a habit of pouring forth "a perfectly wonderful train of disjointed expressions." There is no clear word picture of Nicholas except that his eyes were "bright with the light of intelligence and spirit. His figure was somewhat slight, but manly and well formed; and, apart from the grace of youth and comeliness, there was an emanation from the warm young heart in his look and bearing."

The trio come to London to appeal to the generosity of the deceased father's brother, Ralph Nickleby, a thoroughly villainous conniver and moneylender. He does not propose to support them; the children must work. Perhaps Kate's knowledge of French will make it possible for her to be apprenticed at some boarding school, "or perhaps dress-making or tambour work will come lighter." As to Nicholas, the uncle has brought with him a newspaper containing an advertisement for a boys' school, which closes with the information that a teacher is wanted.

"EDUCATION—At Mr. Wackford Squeers' Academy, Dotheboys Hall, at the delightful village of Dotheboys, near Greta Bridge in Yorkshire. Youth are boarded, clothed, booked, furnished with pocket-money, provided with all necessaries, instructed in all languages living and dead, mathematics, orthography, geometry, astronomy, trigonometry, the use of the globes, algebra, single stick (if required), writing, arithmetic, fortification, and every other branch of classical literature. Terms, twenty guineas per annum. No extras, no vacations, and diet unparalleled. Mr. Squeers is in town, and attends daily, from one till four, at the Saracen's Head, Snow Hill. N.B. An able asisstant wanted. Annual salary £5. A Master of Arts would be preferred."

Nicholas protests that he is not a Master of Arts, but his

uncle assures him that this can be got over. He obviously has some influence with Squeers, upon whom the nephew and uncle wait the next day at the Saracen's Head. While they wait Squeers interviews a Mr. Snawley, who is thinking of placing two boys in this institution. The boys are not his—he married their mother, says Snawley, and "it's expensive keeping boys at home, and as she has a little money in her own right, I am afraid (women are so very foolish, Mr. Squeers) that she might be led to squander it on them, which would be their ruin, you know. . . . and this has made me anxious to put them in some school a good distance off, where there are no holidays—none of those ill-judged comings home twice a year that unsettle children's minds so—and where they may rough it a little—you comprehend?" Squeers comprehends. "Payments regular, and no questions asked," he says, and as to letter writing there is "None, except at Christmas, to say they never were so happy, and hope they never will be sent for."

After Uncle Ralph has a few words aside with Squeers, Nicholas is promptly hired and leaves on the coach for Dotheboys Hall next morning, shepherding three forlorn new students.

Mr. Squeers was not prepossessing in appearance. "He had but one eye, and the popular prejudice runs in favour of two. The eye he had was unquestionably useful, but decidedly not ornamental, being of a greenish grey, and in shape resembling the fan-light of a street door. The blank side of his face was much wrinkled and puckered up, which gave him a very sinister appearance, especially when he smiled, at which times his expression bordered closely on the villainous. His hair was very flat and shiny, save at the ends, where it was brushed stiffly up from a low protruding forehead, which assorted well with his harsh voice and coarse manner. He was about two or three and fifty, and a trifle below the middle size; he wore a white neckerchief with long ends, and a suit of scholastic black; but his coat sleeves being a great deal too long, and his trousers a great deal too short, he appeared ill at ease in his clothes, and as if he were in a perpetual state of astonishment at finding himself so respectable."

Mrs. Squeers, whom Nicholas meets upon his arrival at Dotheboys Hall, is "of a large raw-boned figure, about half a head taller than Mr. Squeers, and was dressed in a dimity night-jacket, with her hair in papers; and she had also a dirty nightcap on, relieved by a yellow cotton handkerchief which tied under the chin." He also meets a retarded youth named Smike, somewhat younger than himself. He learns that Smike had come to the school as a pupil some years before and that his mentor had ceased to pay his bill. Thereafter the simple fellow had become the work horse of the institution in return for shelter and what passed for food.

Nicholas spends the night in a dormitory where the students huddled on the floor. At daybreak he has his first view of his pathetic charges. "It needed a quick eye to detect, from among the huddled mass of sleepers, the form of any given individual. As they lay closely packed together, covered, for warmth's sake, with their patched and ragged clothes, little could be distinguished but the sharp outlines of pale faces, over which the sombre light shed the same dull heavy colour; with, here and there, a gaunt arm thrust forth, its thinness hidden by no covering, but fully exposed to view, in all its shrunken ugliness. There were some who, lying on their backs with upturned faces and clenched hands, just visible in the leaden light, bore more the aspect of dead bodies than of living creatures; and there were others coiled up into strange and fantastic postures, such as might have been taken for the uneasy efforts of pain to gain some temporary relief, rather than the freaks of slumber. A few—and these were among the youngest of the children—slept peacefully on, with smiles upon their faces, dreaming perhaps of home; but ever and again a deep and heavy sigh, breaking the stillness of the room, announced that some new sleeper had awakened to the misery of another day; and, as morning took the place of night, the smiles gradually faded away, with the friendly darkness which had given them birth."

After a morning ceremony in which the boys were "physicked" with treacle by Mrs. Squeers—who, her husband said, was "a mother to them"—the youngsters had a breakfast of "a brown composition which looked like diluted pincushions without the covers, and was called porridge. A minute wedge of brown bread was inserted in each bowl, and when they had eaten their porridge by means of the bread, the boys ate the bread itself, and had finished their breakfast."

The new assistant is next introduced to the unique method of instruction at Dotheboys Hall, a system devised by Squeers that had the great advantage of combining the practical with the theoretical in learning. The headmaster explains it to him as follows:

" 'This is the first class in English spelling and philosophy, Nickleby,' said Squeers, beckoning Nicholas to stand beside him. 'We'll get up a Latin one, and hand that over to you. Now, then, where's the first boy?'

" 'Please, sir, he's cleaning the back parlour window,' said the temporary head of the philosophical class.

" 'So he is, to be sure,' rejoined Squeers. 'We go upon the practical mode of teaching, Nickleby; the regular education system. C-l-e-a-n, clean, verb active, to make bright, to scour. W-i-n, win, d-e-r, winder, a casement. When the boy knows this out of the book, he goes and does it. It's just the same principle as the use of the globes. Where's the second boy?'

"'Please, sir, he's weeding the garden,' replied a small voice.

"'To be sure,' said Squeers, by no means disconcerted. 'So he is. B-o-t, bot, t-i-n, tin bottin, n-e-y, ney bottinney, noun substantive, a knowledge of plants. When he has learned that bottinney means a knowledge of plants, he goes and knows 'em. That's our system, Nickleby; what do you think of it?' "

After lessons—or after all of the boys had completed the chores to which they were assigned in lieu of lessons—Squeers performs a ritual that habitually followed his semi-annual visit to London. He calls all the boys together and gives them messages from their parents or guardians. When there are letters he tells the substance of the communication to the assembled boys:

"'Oh! Cobbey's grandmother is dead, and his Uncle John has took to drinking, which is all the news his sister sends, except eighteenpence, which will pay for that broken square of glass. Mrs. Squeers, my dear, will you take the money?'

"'Graymarsh—he's the next. Stand up, Graymarsh!' "

Another boy stood up.

"'Graymarsh's maternal aunt is very glad to hear he's so well and happy, and sends her respectful compliments to Mrs. Squeers, and thinks she must be an angel. She likewise thinks Mr. Squeers is too good for this world, but hopes he may long be spared to carry on the business. Would have sent the two pair of stockings, as desired, but is short of money, so forwards a tract instead. Hopes, above all things, that Graymarsh will study to please Mr. and Mrs. Squeers, and look upon them as his only friends; and that he will love

Master Squeers; and not object to sleeping five in a bed, which no Christian should. Ah, a delightful letter; very affecting, indeed.'

"It was affecting in one sense; for Graymarsh's maternal aunt was strongly supposed by her more intimate friends to be his maternal parent.

" 'Mobbs' mother-in-law took to her bed on hearing that he wouldn't eat fat, and has been very ill ever since. She wishes to know by an early post where he expects to go to, if he quarrels with his vittles; and with what feelings he *could* turn up his nose at the cow's-liver broth, after his good master had asked a blessing on it. This was told her in the London newspapers—not by Mr. Squeers, for he is too kind and too good to set anybody against anybody. Mobbs' mother-in-law is sorry to find Mobbs is discontented (which is sinful and horrid), and hopes Mr. Squeers will flog him into a happier state of mind; with this view she has also stopped his halfpenny a week pocket-money, and given a double-bladed knife, with a corkscrew in it, which she had bought on purpose for him, to the missionaries. A sulky state of feeling won't do. Cheerfulness and contentment must be kept up. —Mobbs, come to me!' "

"The unhappy Mobbs moved slowly towards the desk, rubbing his eyes in anticipation of good cause for doing so; and soon afterwards retired by the side door, with as good cause as a boy need have."

Nicholas had treated the wretched Smike kindly since their first meeting and this unfortunate creature—who could not remember ever having been the subject of sympathy before—attaches himself to the young teacher with doglike devotion. The result was to make Smike's miserable life even harder. Mrs. Squeers had taken an instant dislike to Nicholas; Miss

Fanny Squeers, the daughter, had become vindictive when Nicholas spurned her proffered passion; Mr. Squeers was jealous of his assistant's relationship with his drudge. All of these vent their venom on Smike until the poor youth runs away.

He is brought back the next day, tied hand and foot in a wagon, and Squeers starts to give him a cruel beating before the assembled school, for which he has specially procured a new whip. When Nicholas intervenes and orders him to stop, Squeers takes a cut at his assistant, at which the youth loses his head and beats the headmaster into insensibility. He then packs his meager belongings and leaves the school with no definite destination in mind. When he awakes in a barn the next morning he finds Smike standing over him. The devoted youngster stays with Nicholas until, late in the book, he dies of tuberculosis.

This section about Dotheboys Hall was the *raison d'être* for the novel *Nicholas Nickleby*, although it is entirely contained in the first sixth of the book. The dastardly Squeers reappears repeatedly throughout the story, trying to harm Nicholas and regain custody of Smike (who turns out to be uncle Ralph's illegitimate son). Because Dickens never left any loose ends, the story returns to Dotheboys Hall at the very end of the book. By this time Squeers is in jail.

"The news of Mr. Squeers' downfall had reached Dotheboys; that was quite clear. To all appearance, it had very recently become known to the young gentlemen, for rebellion had just broken out.

"It was one of the brimstone-and-treacle mornings, and Mrs. Squeers had entered school according to custom with the large bowl and spoon, followed by Miss Squeers and the amiable Wackford, [Squeers' teen-age son] who, during his father's absence, had taken upon himself such minor branches of the executive as kicking the pupils with his nailed boots, pulling the hair of some of the smaller boys, pinching the others in aggravating places, and rendering himself in various ways a great comfort and happiness to his mother. Their entrance, whether by premeditation or a simultaneous impulse, was the signal for revolt. While one detachment rushed to the door and locked it, and another mounted the desks and forms, the stoutest (and consequently the newest) boy seized the cane, and confronting Mrs. Squeers with a stern countenance, snatched off her cap and beaver-bonnet, put it on his own head, armed himself with the wooden spoon and bade her, on pain of death, go down upon her knees and take a dose directly. Before that estimable lady could recover herself, or offer the slightest retaliation, she was forced into a kneeling posture by a crowd of shouting tormentors, and compelled to swallow a spoonful of the odious mixture, rendered more than usually savoury by the immersion in the bowl of Master Wackford's head, whose ducking was entrusted to another rebel. The success of this first achievement prompted the malicious crowd, whose faces were clustered together in every variety of lank and half-starved ugliness, to further acts of outrage."

An account of Dotheboys Hall and the reprehensible Squeers should include a letter that Dickens wrote to a five-year-old critic, if only to show how the author could enter into the world of childish fancies. Like other Dickens novels *Nicholas Nickleby* originally ran as a magazine serial, the opening installments of which were read to Master Hastings Hughes by his father. As the story progressed without the Squeers family being properly punished—Squeers' downfall came late in the novel—young Master Hughes felt that justice had not been done. He believed that the Squeers family should be made to suffer for their evil doings and that their victims should be in some way compensated. He dictated a letter to his father suggesting how this could be accomplished and how the novel should conclude. Dickens replied:

Respected Sir,

I have given Squeers one cut on the neck and two on the head, at which he appeared much surprised and began to cry, which, being a cowardly thing, is just what I should have expected from him—wouldn't you?

I have carefully done what you told me in your letter about the lamb and the two 'sheeps' for the little boys. They have also had some good ale and porter, and some wine. I am sorry you didn't say *what* wine you would like them to have. I gave them some sherry, which they liked very much; except one boy, who was a little sick and choked a good deal. He was rather greedy, and that's the truth, and I believe it went the wrong way, which I say served him right, and I hope you will say so too.

Nicholas had his roast lamb, as you said he was to, but he could not eat it all, and says if you do not mind his doing so he should like to have the rest hashed tomorrow with some greens, which he is very fond of, and so am I. He said he did not like to have his porter hot, for he thought it spoilt the flavour, so I let him have it cold. You should have seen him drink it. I thought he never would have left off. I also gave him three pounds of money, all in sixpences, to make it seem more, and he said directly that he should give more than half to his mamma and sister, and divide the rest with poor Smike. And I say he is a good fellow for saying so; and if anybody says he isn't I am ready to fight him whenever they like—there!

Fanny Squeers shall be attended to, depend upon it. Your

drawing of her is very like, except that I don't think the hair
is quite curly enough. The nose is particularly like hers, and
so are the legs. She is a nasty disagreeable thing, and I know
it will make her very cross when she sees it; and what I say
is that I hope it may.

In the novel *Dombey and Son* Dickens sends his youthful
characters to three schools, all very different and all subject to
the writer's disapproval for one reason or another. When
Paul Dombey is an infant his father rewards his wet nurse,
Richards, by nominating her young son to a charity school.
In informing the nurse of his generosity, Mr. Dombey makes
clear his views on education for the masses:

" 'I am far from being friendly,' pursued Mr. Dombey, 'to
what is called by persons of levelling sentiments, general
education. But it is necessary that the inferior classes should
continue to be taught to know their position, and to conduct
themselves properly. So far I approve of schools. Having the
power of nominating a child on the foundation of an ancient
establishment, called (from a worshipful company) the
Charitable Grinders, where not only is a wholesome education bestowed upon the scholars, but where a dress and badge
is likewise provided for them, I have . . . nominated your
eldest son to an existing vacancy; and he has this day, I am
informed, assumed the habit. The number of her son, I believe,' said Mr. Dombey, turning to his sister and speaking
of the child as if he were a hackney coach, 'is one hundred
and forty-seven, Louisa, you can tell her.'

" 'One hundred and forty-seven,' said Mrs. Chick. 'The
dress, Richards, is a nice, warm, blue baize tailed coat and
cap, turned up with orange-coloured binding; red worsted
stockings; and very strong leather small-clothes. One might

wear the articles one's-self,' said Mrs. Chick, with enthusiasm, 'and be grateful.' "

Dickens himself had no such respect nor admiration for the uniform that labeled a child an object of charity and he detailed the new scholar's woes as follows:

"Now, it happened that poor Biler's life had been, since yesterday morning, rendered weary by the costume of the Charitable Grinders. The youth of the streets could not endure it. No young vagabond could be brought to bear its contemplation for a moment, without throwing himself upon the unoffending wearer, and doing him mischief. His social existence had been more like that of an early Christian than an innocent child of the nineteenth century. He had been stoned in the streets. He had been overthrown into gutters, bespattered with mud, violently flattened against posts. Entire strangers to his person had lifted his yellow cap off his head and cast it to the winds. His legs had not only undergone verbal criticisms and revilings, but had been handled and pinched. That very morning, he had received a perfectly unsolicited black eye on his way to the Grinders' establishment, and had been punished for it by the master."

Young Biler went to the same type of educational institution as those attended by Uriah Heep in *David Copperfield* and Noah Claypole in *Oliver Twist*. The former, and his father before him, learned "a good deal of 'umbleness" and not much else, at a charity school, both of them even earning "the monitor-medal for being 'umble." When David Copperfield hears this he realizes, for the first time, that "this despicable cant of false humility might have originated out of the Heep family. I had seen the harvest, but never thought of the seed." In the case of Noah Claypole, his role as a bully is traced to the charity school. He revenges himself on Oliver for the taunts of "leathers," "charity," and the like that he had to endure while wearing the uniform.

Biler (whose right name was Robin Toodles) claimed that his career of "wagging" or truancy, and the bad ways and evil companionship to which this led, started with the terrors of his journey to school in the hated uniform and the ritual floggings that he received when he got there. His father, distressed at his going to the bad, suggests to Mr. Dombey that the boy, "huffed and cuffed, and flogged and badgered, and taught, as parrots are, by a brute jobbed into his place of schoolmaster with as much fitness for it as a hound, might not have been educated on quite a right plan in some undiscovered respect."

The second school in *Dombey and Son* is the Infantile Boarding Establishment run by Mrs. Pipchin that has been previously mentioned. Paul entered this institution when he was five years old and stayed for about a year. Then his father felt that he was old enough to undertake the type of education that would prepare him to take his rightful place in the banking house of Dombey and Son. The lad was sent to a select and expensive boys boarding school run by Dr. Blimber.

"Whenever a young gentleman was taken in hand by Doctor Blimber, he might consider himself sure of a pretty tight squeeze. The Doctor only undertook the charge of ten young gentlemen, but he had, always ready, a supply of learning for a hundred, on the lowest estimate; and it was at once the business and delight of his life to gorge the unhappy ten with it.

"In fact, Doctor Blimber's establishment was a great hothouse, in which there was a forcing apparatus incessantly at work. All the boys blew before their time. Mental green-peas were produced at Christmas, and intellectual asparagus all the year round. Mathematical gooseberries (very sour ones, too) were common at untimely seasons, and from mere sprouts of bushes, under Doctor Blimber's cultivation. Every description of Greek and Latin vegetable was got off the driest twigs of boys, under the frostiest circumstances. Nature was of no consequence at all. No matter what a young gentleman was intended to bear, Doctor Blimber made him bear to pattern, somehow or other."

Dr. Blimber was assisted by his daughter, who was "dry and sandy from working in the graves of dead languages. None of your live languages for Miss Blimber. They must be dead—stone dead—and then Miss Blimber dug them up like a ghoul." Mrs. Blimber was not learned herself, but she had great respect for learning and always said, at dinner parties, "that if she could have known Cicero, she thought she could have died contented." It was the steady joy of her life to see the Doctor's young gentlemen go out walking, "unlike all other young gentlemen, in the largest possible shirt-collars, and the stiffest possible cravats, it was so classical, she said."

Under the forced feeding system employed at Dr. Blimber's, "The young gentlemen were prematurely full of corking anxieties. They knew no rest from the pursuit of stone-hearted verbs, savage noun-substantives, inflexible syntactic passages, and ghosts of exercises that appeared to them in their dreams. Under the forcing system, a young gentleman usually took leave of his spirits in three weeks. He had all the cares of the world on his head in three months. He conceived bitter sentiments against his parents or guardians in four; he was an old misanthrope, in five; envied Curtius that blessed refuge in the earth, in six; and at the end of the first twelve months had arrived at the conclusion, from which he never afterwards departed, that all the fancies of the poets, and lessons of the sages, were a mere collection of words and grammar, and had no other meaning in the world."

The most amusing product of Dr. Blimber's school was Toots, the oldest of the boys. Toots had "gone through" everything and had "suddenly left off blowing one day and remained in the establishment as a mere stalk. And people did say that the Doctor had rather overdone it with young Toots, and that when he began to have whiskers he left off having brains." When the boys went for their daily walk Toots stealthily donned a ring that he kept in his waistcoat pocket and was "constantly falling in love with nursemaids, who had no idea of his existence." Having gone through so much, Toots had license to pursue his own course of studies, "which was chiefly to write long letters to himself from persons of distinction, addressed 'P. Toots, Esquire, Brighton, Sussex,' and preserve them in his desk with great care."

In the novel *Hard Times* a school supported by Mr. Gradgrind, a big man in wholesale hardware, and conducted by Mr. M'Choakumchild, the schoolmaster, is the poor man's equivalent of Dr. Blimber's establishment. *Hard Times* is an account of the English industrial society of the day and the philosophy of those who sustained it, but the account centers on the corrupting influence of that philosophy on children. Gradgrindery is in every way utilitarian, ignoring completely the life of the spirit.

Mr. Gradgrind is a good father to the five little Gradgrinds, after his fashion. He has instructed them himself long before they ever went to school. "They had been lectured at, from their tenderest years; coursed, like little hares. Almost as soon as they could run alone, they had been made to run to the lecture-room. The first object with which they had an association, or of which they had a remembrance, was a large blackboard with a dry Ogre chalking ghastly white figures on it.

"Not that they knew, by name or nature, anything about an Ogre. Fact forbid! I only use the word to express a monster in a lecturing castle, with Heaven knows how many heads manipulated into one, taking childhood captive, and dragging it into gloomy statistical dens by the hair.

"No little Gradgrind had ever seen a face in the moon; it was up in the moon before it could speak distinctly. No little Gradgrind was ever learnt the silly jingle, 'Twinkle, Twinkle, little star; how I wonder what you are!' No little Gradgrind had ever known wonder on the subject, each little Gradgrind having at five years old dissected the Great Bear like a Professor Own, and driven Charles's Wain like a locomotive engine-driver. No little Gradgrind had ever associated a cow in a field with that famous cow with the crumpled horn who tossed the dog who worried the cat who killed the rat who ate the malt, or with that yet more famous cow who swallowed Tom Thumb. It had never heard of those celebrities, and had only been introduced to a cow as a graminivorous ruminating quadruped with several stomachs."

Mr. Gradgrind's educational philosophy produces an older son who becomes a gambler and a bank robber, and a daughter who makes an unhappy marriage, falls in love with another man, and has the nearest thing to an illicit affair that one will find in Dickens—her lover puts his arm around her. The daughter, Louisa, flies from her husband and returns to her father, crying, "Father, your philosophy and your teaching will not save me. Save me by some other means." Gradgrind has no other means of saving his daughter, but he does realize the blight that he has brought on the lives of his children by trying to put aside the spirit of childhood. The underlying motivation of *Hard Times* is identical with that of *Dombey and Son.*

Hard Times is a crusade against the economic system of mid-nineteenth-century England, but it starts in a school. This institution Dickens condemns in that its administrators are concerned solely with the verities of the academic subjects in the curriculum—they have no time or sympathy for childish imagery, such must be driven from youthful heads and replaced by inexorable logic. In lampooning this type of education Dickens, three quarters of a century before their time, was expressing the basic idea of the twentieth-century progressive educators who decry traditional schooling because it is subject oriented rather than child oriented.

In the opening pages of the book Mr. Gradgrind and a government official have arrived to inspect the institiution, and the former makes clear his theories of education in the opening words of the novel by saying:

"Now, what I want is, Facts. Teach these boys and girls nothing but Facts. Facts alone are wanted in life. Plant nothing else, and root out everything else. You can only form the minds of reasoning animals upon Facts: nothing else will ever be of any service to them. This is the principle on which I bring up my own children, and this is the principle on which I bring up these children. Stick to Facts, sir!"

As Mr. Gradgrind stands before the class with the official and the schoolmaster, Dickens describes him as "a kind of cannon loaded to the muzzle with facts, and prepared to blow them clean out of the regions of childhood at one discharge. He seemed a galvanizing apparatus, too, charged with a grim mechanical substitute for the tender young imaginations that were to be stormed away.

" 'Girl number twenty,' said Mr. Gradgrind, squarely pointing with his square forefinger, 'I don't know that girl. Who is that girl?'

" 'Sissy Jupe, sir,' explained number twenty, blushing, standing up, and curtseying.

" 'Sissy is not a name," said Mr. Gradgrind. 'Don't call yourself Sissy. Call yourself Cecelia.'

" 'It's father as calls me Sissy, sir,' returned the young girl in a trembling voice, and with another curtsey.

" 'Then he has no business to do it,' said Mr. Gradgrind. 'Tell him he mustn't. Cecelia Jupe. Let me see. What is your father?' "

Sissy haltingly explains that her father "belongs to the horse riding," and her interrogator elicits that he breaks, shoes, and doctors horses. Mr. Gradgrind then asks the girl to define a horse, and the child is "thrown into the greatest alarm by this demand."

" 'Girl number twenty unable to define a horse!' said Mr. Gradgrind, for the general behoof of all the little pitchers. 'Girl number twenty possessed of no facts, in reference to one of the commonest of animals! Some boy's definition of a horse ...'

" 'Bitzer,' said Thomas Gradgrind. 'Your definition of a horse.'

" 'Quadruped, graminivorous. Forty teeth, namely twenty-four grinders, four eye-teeth, and twelve incisive. Sheds coat in the spring; in marshy countries, sheds hoofs, too. Hoofs hard, but requiring to be shod with iron. Age known by marks in mouth.' Thus (and much more) Bitzer.

" 'Now girl number twenty,' said Mr. Gradgrind. 'You know what a horse is.'

"She curtseyed again, and would have blushed deeper, if

she could have blushed deeper than she had blushed all this
time. Bitzer, after rapidly blinking at Thomas Gradgrind
with both eyes at once, and so catching the light upon his
quivering ends of lashes that they looked like the antennae of
busy insects, put his knuckles to his freckled forehead, and
sat down again."

The government official now took up the questioning:
" 'Very well,' said this gentleman, briskly smiling, and
folding his arms. 'That's a horse. Now, let me ask you girls
and boys, would you paper a room with representations of
horses?'

"After a pause, one half of the children cried in chorus,
'Yes, Sir!' Upon which the other half, seeing in the gentle-
man's face that Yes was wrong, cried out in chorus, "No,
Sir!'—as the custom is, in these examinations.

" 'Of course, No. Why wouldn't you?'

"A pause. One corpulent slow boy, with a wheezy manner
of breathing, ventured the answer: 'Because I wouldn't paper a room at all, but would paint it.'

" 'You *must* paper it,' said the gentleman, rather warmly.

" 'You must paper it,' said Thomas Gradgrind, 'whether
you like it or not. Don't tell *us* you wouldn't paper it. What
do you mean, boy?'

" 'I'll explain to you, then,' said the gentleman, after another and a dismal pause, 'why you wouldn't paper a room
with representations of horses. Do you ever see horses walking up and down the sides of rooms in reality—in fact? Do
you?'

" 'Yes, Sir!' from one half, 'No, Sir!' from the other.

" 'Of course, No,' said the gentleman, with an indignant
look at the wrong half. 'Why, then you are not to see anywhere, what you don't see in fact; you are not to have any-

where, what you don't have in fact. What is called Taste, is only another name for Fact.'

"Thomas Gradgrind nodded his approbation.

" 'This is a new principle, a discovery, a great discovery,' said the gentleman. 'Now, I'll try you again. Suppose you were going to carpet a room. Would you use a carpet having a representation of flowers upon it?'

"There being a general conviction by this time that 'No, Sir!' was always the right answer to this gentleman, the chorus of No was very strong. Only a few feeble stragglers said Yes, among them Sissy Jupe.

" 'Girl number twenty,' said the gentleman, smiling in the calm strength of knowledge.

"Sissy blushed and stood up.

" 'So you would carpet your room—or your husband's room if you were a grown woman, and had a husband—with representations of flowers, would you?' said the gentleman. 'Why would you?'

" 'If you please, sir, I am very fond of flowers,' returned the girl.

" 'And is that why you would put tables and chairs upon them, and have people walking over them with heavy boots?'

" 'It wouldn't hurt them, sir. They wouldn't crush and wither, if you please, sir. They would be the pictures of what was very pretty and pleasant, and I would fancy——'

" 'Ay, ay, ay! But you mustn't fancy,' cried the gentleman, quite elated by coming so happily to his point. 'That's it! You are never to fancy. . . . You must discard the word Fancy altogether. You have nothing to do with it. You are not to have, in any object of use or ornament, what would be a contradiction in fact. You don't walk upon flowers in fact; you cannot be allowed to walk upon flowers in carpets.

You don't find that foreign birds and butterflies come and perch upon your crockery; you cannot be permitted to paint foreign birds and butterflies upon your crockery. You never meet with quadurpeds going up and down walls; you must not have quadrupeds represented upon walls. You must see,' said the gentleman, 'for all these purposes, combinations and modifications (in primary colours) of mathematical figures which are susceptible of proof and demonstration. This is the new discovery. This is Fact. This is Taste.' "

In his earlier novels Dickens had repeatedly castigated the ignorant schoolmaster. By the time that *Hard Times* started to run serially in "Household Words" in April 1854, teacher-training colleges had come into existence, and the first batch of Queen's Scholars had emerged as teachers in the previous year. Mr. M'Choakumchild is presumably one of these. They had not yet had an opportunity to demonstrate the merits of their training, and Dickens, based on his previous criticism of lack of teacher-training, should presumably have favored any effort in this direction, yet he presented M'Choakumchild and his training entirely from a satirical point of view.

"He and some one hundred and forty other schoolmasters had been lately turned at the same time, in the same factory, on the same principles, like so many pianoforte legs. He had been put through an immense variety of paces, and had answered volumes of head-breaking questions. Orthography, etymology, syntax, and prosody, biography, astronomy, geography, and general cosmography, the sciences of compound proportion, algebra, land-surveying and levelling, vocal music, and drawing from models, were all at the ends of his ten chilled fingers. He had worked his stony way into Her Majesty's most Honourable Privy Council's Schedule B, and had taken the bloom off the higher branches of mathematics and physical science, French, German, Latin, and Greek. He knew all about all the Watersheds of all the world (whatever they are), and all the histories of all the peoples, and all the names of all the rivers and mountains, and all the productions, manners, and customs of all the countries, and all their boundaries and bearings on the two-and-thirty points of the compass. Ah, rather overdone, M'Choakumchild. If he had only learnt a little less, how definitely better he might have taught much more!"

Of a piece with schoolteacher M'Choakumchild in *Hard Times* was pedant Bradley Headstone, conceived ten years later in *Our Mutual Friend*. It is obvious that Dickens still did not approve of the trained teachers of the times, for of Bradley Headstone's preparation for his profession he wrote:

"He had acquired mechanically a great store of teacher's knowledge. He could do mental arithmetic mechanically, sing at sight mechanically, blow various wind instruments mechanically, even play the great church organ mechanically. From his early childhood up, his mind had been a place of mechanical stowage. The arrangement of his wholesale warehouse, so that it might be always ready to meet the demands of retail dealers—history here, geography there, astronomy to the right, political economy to the left—natural history, the physical sciences, figures, music, the lower mathematics, and what not, all in their several places—this care had imparted to his countenance a look of care; while the habit of questioning and being questioned had given him a suspicious manner, or a manner that would be better described as one of lying in wait. There was a kind of settled trouble in the face. . . . He always seemed to be uneasy lest anything should be missing from his mental warehouse, and taking stock to assure himself."

Dickens wrote nothing about the school that Bradley Headstone conducted; the teacher was a principal in the plot of the novel rather than merely an incidental schoolteacher. But the novelist did describe the school from which Headstone had taken one of the other characters in the book, Charley Hexam. His notes on the novel refer to this as a "Ragged School," although it is not so labeled in the book, where it was described as: "The school at which young Charley Hexam had first learned from a book—the streets being, for pupils of his degree, the great Preparatory Establishment in which very much that is never unlearned is learned without and before books—was a miserable loft in an unsavory yard. Its atmosphere was oppressive and disagreeable; it was crowded, noisy, and confusing; half the pupils dropped asleep, or fell into a state of waking stupefaction; the other half kept them in either condition by maintaining a monotonous droning noise, as if they were performing out of time and tune, on a ruder sort of bagpipe. . . . All the place was pervaded by a grimly ludicrous pretense that every pupil was childish and innocent. This pretense, much favored by the lady visitors, led to the ghastliest absurdities. Young women old in the vices of the commonest and worst life, were expected to profess themselves enthralled by the good child's book, the *Adventures of Little Margery*, who . . . severely reproved and morally squashed the miller, when she was five and he was fifty."

Some of Dickens' principal child characters did not go to school—Little Nell in *Old Curiosity Shop* was one. This poor child was so busy taking care of her aged grandfather that she had little time for anything else. But Dickens did take occasion in this novel to castigate girls' finishing schools with their perverted morality, snobbish gentility, and emphasis on useless "feminine accomplishments." When Nell is working in a traveling waxworks the proprietor, Mrs. Jarley, is distressed because at a certain stop only eight of Miss Monflathers' young ladies have attended the display. Little Nell is sent to deliver circulars to Miss Monflathers' school to attract better attendance:

"Nell had no difficulty in finding out Miss Monflathers's Boarding and Day Establishment, which was a large house, with a high wall, and a large garden-gate with a large brass plate, and a small grating through which Miss Monflathers's parlour-maid inspected all visitors before admitting them; for nothing in the shape of a man—no, not even a milkman—was suffered, without special license, to pass that gate. Even the tax-gatherer, who was stout, and wore spectacles and a broad-brimmed hat, had the taxes handed through the grating. More obdurate than gate of adamant or brass, this gate of Miss Monflathers's frowned on all mankind. The very butcher respected it as a gate of mystery, and left off whistling when he rang the bell."

As Nell approaches the school she meets a procession of young ladies coming out for their daily walk, shepherded by Miss Monflathers and two subordinate teachers. The schoolmistress tells Nell that it is "very naughty and unfeminine" to be a waxwork child instead of improving her mind "by the constant contemplation of the steam-engine . . . and earning a comfortable and independent subsistence of from two-and-ninepence to three shillings per week," and she asks: " 'Don't you know that the harder you are at work, the happier you are?'

" 'How doth the little ——' murmured one of the teachers, in quotation from Dr. Watts. . . .

" 'The little busy bee,' said Miss Monflathers, drawing herself up, 'is applicable only to genteel children. In books, or work, or healthful play, it is quite right as far as they are concerned, and the work means painting on velvet, fancy needlework, or embroidery. In such cases as these,' pointing to Nell, with her parasol, 'and in the case of all poor people's children, we should read it thus:

> In work, work, work, in work alway
>   Let my first years be past,
> That I may give for ev'ry day
>   Some good account at last.' "

Particularly in his later novels Dickens more often expressed his disapproval of female education by poking fun at certain of its aspects than by bitter condemnation. His schoolmistresses became less stern and vicious and totally incompetent. Miss Twinkleton, who ran a Seminary for Young Ladies in his last, unfinished novel, *Edwin Drood,* was a kindly, sympathetic character who exists in a flutter of gentility and prudery. But Miss Twinkleton has fixed ideas on what is suitable literature for young ladies, as becomes evident when she reads aloud to her pupil, Rosa Bud. Rosa soon discovers that "she didn't read fairly."

"She cut the love scenes, interpolated passages in praise of female celibacy, and was guilty of other glaring pious frauds. As an instance in point, take the glowing passage: 'Ever dearest and best adored,'—said Edward, clasping the dear head to his breast, and drawing the silken hair through his caressing fingers, from which he suffered it to fall like golden rain—'ever dearest and best adored, let us fly from the unsympathetic world and the sterile coldness of the stony-hearted, to the rich warm Paradise of Trust and Love.' Miss Twinkleton's fraudulent version tamely ran thus: 'Ever engaged to me with the consent of our parents on both sides, and the approbation of the silver-haired rector of the district,'—said Edward, respectfully raising to his lips the tapered fingers so skillful in embroidery, tambour, crochet, and other truly feminine arts—'let me call on thy papa ere to-morrow's dawn has sunk into the west, and propose a suburban establishment, lowly it may be, but within our means, where he will be always welcome as an evening guest, and where every arrangement shall invest economy, and constant interchange of scholastic acquirements, with the attributes of the ministering angel to domestic bliss.' "

Almost all the characters in Dickens' novels who are shown getting an education are the worse for it, emotionally and morally, because of the type of education they get. But the few characters who receive a better education do not particularly benefit from it in terms of a richer life. They merely attain a more respectable place in society and tolerably well-paid jobs.

Dickens wrote brilliantly, caustically, humorously, satirically, and convincingly about bad schools of many shapes and forms. He was far less compelling when he tried to describe the one school in all of his novels that he endorsed as a good school. This was Dr. Strong's establishment in *David Copperfield*, to which David went as a teen-ager. Of this institution he had David say:

"Doctor Strong's was an excellent school, as different from Mr. Creakle's as good is from evil. It was very gravely and decorously ordered, and on a sound system, with an appeal, in everything, to the honour and good faith of the boys, and an avowed intention to rely on their possession of those qualities unless they proved themselves unworthy of it, which

worked wonders. We all felt that we had a part in the management of the place, and in sustaining its character and dignity. Hence, we soon became warmly attached to it—I am
sure I did for one, and I never knew, in all my time, of any
other boy being otherwise—and learnt with a good will,
desiring to do it credit. We had noble games out of hours,
and plenty of liberty; but even then, as I remember, we were
well spoken of in the town, and rarely did any disgrace, by
our appearance or manner, to the reputation of Doctor
Strong and Doctor Strong's boys."

Dr. Strong's school occupied "a grave building in a court-
yard, with a learned air about." When David arrived in the
dignified classroom he found his new schoolmates "studiously
engaged at their books." They rose politely when Dr. Strong
brought him in and the head boy, "very affable and good
humoured," welcomed him and introduced him "in a gentle-
manly way." Dr. Strong himself was a prototype of the
absent-minded professor of comic legend, but he possessed a
sweet amiability, an endearing simplicity and was "the least
suspicious of mankind." When Philip Toynbee discussed
him he remarked: "We are on the road to Mr. Chips."

Dickens says that the school was conducted "on a sound
system," but never tells what the system was. He tells no
anecdotes of David's career in this school; says nothing about
the aspects of school life that would make it memorable to the
teen-age David. The students played at "noble games," but
their nature is unspecified. All that the reader can gather from
the meager description is that Dickens' idea of a good school
is a very progressive school for that time and place. The boys
had "plenty of liberty" and played a part "in the management
of the place, and in sustaining its character and dignity."

CHAPTER

VI

SOME SERVANT GIRLS
AND OTHERS

In the whole galaxy of youth presented in the novels of
Dickens, those juveniles who play important roles in the
stories are but a few stars. Many more youngsters contribute
to the story lines of the various books without playing principal roles, and there are incidental children everywhere un-
derfoot, sometimes put into the books to make crusading or
philosophical points, more often merely for fun. Dickens
liked to write about children. Whereas other authors of the
era studiously ignored children even as incidentals in their
books, perhaps seeing nothing of interest in them, Dickens
sprinkled them everywhere.

Many of these subordinate or incidental children were
servants. These he could easily draw from life because in
Victorian England many, perhaps most, servants were teen-
agers, and little slaveys as young as twelve were not unusual.

One such whom Dickens introduced into *Pickwick Papers* for fun was Joe the Fat Boy, Mr. Wardle's servant who, when not eating, repeatedly fell asleep:

" 'Damn that boy,' said the old gentleman, 'he's gone to sleep again.'

" 'Very extraordinary boy, that,' said Mr. Pickwick. 'Does he always sleep in this way?'

" 'Sleep!' said the old gentleman. 'He's always asleep. Goes on errands fast asleep, and snores as he waits at table.'

" 'How very odd!' said Mr. Pickwick.

" 'Ah! Odd indeed,' returned the old gentleman. 'I'm proud of that boy—wouldn't part with him on any account—he's a natural curiosity! Here, Joe—Joe—take these things away, and open another bottle—d'ye hear?'

"The Fat Boy rose, opened his eyes, swallowed the huge piece of pie he had been in the act of masticating when he last fell asleep, and slowly obeyed his master's orders—gloating languidly over the remains of the feast, as he removed the plates."

Another juvenile in *Pickwick Papers* who was just for fun, was the child who swallowed the necklace. Jack Hopkins, a medical student, told the Pickwickians about him:

" '. . . Child's parents were poor people who lived in a court. Child's eldest sister bought a necklace—common necklace, made of large black wooden beads. Child, being fond of toys, cribbed the necklace, hid it, played with it, cut the string, and swallowed a bead. Child thought it capital fun; went back next day, and swallowed another bead.'

" 'Bless my heart,' said Mr. Pickwick, 'what a dreadful thing! I beg your pardon, sir. Go on.'

" 'Next day, child swallowed two beads; the day after that, he treated himself to three; and so on, till in a week's time he had got through the necklace—five-and-twenty beads in all. The sister, who was an industrious girl and seldom treated herself to a bit of finery, cried her eyes out at the loss of the necklace; looked high and low for it; but, I needn't say, didn't find it. A few days after, the family were at dinner; the child, who wasn't hungry, was playing about the room, when suddenly there was heard a devil of a noise, like a small hailstorm. "Don't do that, my boy," said the father. "I ain't a doin' nothin'," said the child. "Well, don't do it again," said the father; "you'll find yourself in bed in something less than a pig's whisper." He gave the child a shake to make him obedient; and such a rattling ensued as nobody ever heard before. "Why damme, it's *in* the child!" said the father. "He's got the croup in the wrong place."

"'"No, I haven't, father," said the child, beginning to cry. "It's the necklace: I swallowed it, father."'' "The father caught the child up, and ran with him to the hospital; the beads in the boy's stomach rattling all the way with the jolting, and the people looking up in the air, and down in the cellars, to see where the unusual sound came from. 'He's in the hospital now,' said Jack Hopkins, 'and he makes such a devil of a noise when he walks about that they're obliged to muffle him in a watchman's coat, for fear he should wake the patients.'"

There is a large gallery of young female servants in Dickens' novels, some purely incidental, others who play some small part in the story. The most prominent girls in this category are the Orfling in *David Copperfield*, the Marchioness and Barbara in *Old Curiosity Shop*, Susan Nipper in *Dombey and Son*, and Tattycoram in *Little Dorrit*. Of these the one who might come first in the category is the Marchioness, because she is not only an interesting character in herself but is involved in the working out of the plot of the novel.

The Marchioness works for attorney Sampson Brass and his sister Sally, two of the villains of the book. A guess puts her age at thirteen—it has to be a guess because she does not know her name or where she came from. Dick Swiveller is a clerk for Brass and it is he who gives the Marchioness her name. The girl makes her first appearance when Dick is working alone in the office and hears a timid knock at the door of the room. The door is then opened and he hears:

" 'Oh, please,' said a little voice, very low down in the doorway, 'will you come and show the lodgings?'

"Dick leant over the table, and descried a small slipshod girl in a dirty coarse apron and bib, which left nothing of her visible but her face and feet. She might as well have been dressed in a violin-case.

" 'Why, who are you?' said Dick.

"To which the only reply was: 'Oh, please will you come and show the lodgings?'

"There never was such an old-fashioned child in her looks and manner. She must have been at work from her cradle. She seemed as much afraid of Dick, as Dick was amazed at her.

" 'I hav'n't got anything to do with the lodgings,' said Dick. 'Tell 'em to call again.'

" 'Oh, but please will you come and show the lodgings?' returned the girl; 'it's eighteen shillings a week and us finding plate and linen. Boots and clothes is extra, and fires in winter-time is eightpence a day.'

" 'Why don't you show 'em yourself? You seem to know all about 'em,' said Dick.

" 'Miss Sally said I wasn't to, because people wouldn't be-

lieve the attendance was good if they saw how small I was
first.'

" 'Well, but they'll see how small you are afterwards, won't
they?' said Dick.

" 'Ah! But then they'll have taken 'em for a fortnight
certain,' replied the child with a shrewd look; 'and people
don't like moving when they're once settled.'

" 'This is a queer sort of thing,' muttered Dick, rising.
'What do you mean to say you are—the cook?'

" 'Yes, I do plain cooking,' replied the child. 'I'm house-
maid too; I do all the work of the house.' "

Dick becomes fascinated by the mystery of the little slavey
who always remains "somewhere in the bowels of the earth."
Solely out of curiosity he wants to know more about her, but
does not know how to even talk to her. "She never went out,
or came into the office, or had a clean face, or took off the
coarse apron, or looked out of any one of the windows, or
stood at the street-door for a breath of air, or had any rest or
enjoyment whatever. Nobody ever came to see her, nobody
spoke of her, nobody cared about her. Mr. Brass had said
once that he believed she was a "love-child" (which means
anything but a child of love), and that was all the information
Richard Swiveller could obtain."

The Marchioness to this point has no name. When asked,
"Where do you come from?" she replies, "I don't know."

" 'What's your name?'

" 'Nothing.'

" 'Nonsense, what does your mistress call you when she
wants you?'

" 'A little devil,' said the child."

Swiveller is in the habit of playing cribbage with himself
in the evening after work when the Brasses have gone out—

sometimes for fifty thousand pounds a side. One night he hears "a kind of snorting or hard-breathing sound in the direction of the door, which it occurred to him, after some reflection, must proceed from the small servant, who always had a cold from damp living." Glancing at the door he sees an eye gleaming and glistening at the keyhole. Throwing the door open he discloses the small servant. She assures him: "I didn't mean any harm, indeed, upon my word I didn't. . . . It's so very dull downstairs. Please don't tell upon me, please don't." Dick invites the girl in and offers to teach her to play cribbage, but the girl shrinks back, saying, "Miss Sally 'ud kill me if she know'd I come up here." Dick tells her that Miss Sally cannot kill him for going downstairs and goes with the girl to the kitchen, first detouring to the public house next door to get a heaping plate of meat and bread for the half-starved child and a great pot of beer, which the girl had never tasted. "These preliminaries disposed of, he applied himself to teaching her the game, which she soon learnt tolerably well, being both sharp-witted and cunning.

" 'Now,' said Mr. Swiveller, putting two sixpences into a saucer and trimming the wretched candle, when the cards had been cut and dealt, 'those are the stakes. If you win, you get 'em all. If I win, I get 'em. To make it seem more real and pleasant, I shall call you the Marchioness, do you hear?'

"The small servant nodded.

" 'Then Marchioness,' said Mr. Swiveller, 'fire away!'

"The Marchioness, holding her cards very tight in both hands, considered which to play, and Mr. Swiveller, assuming the gay and fashionable air which such society required, took another pull at the tankard, and waited for her lead."

Sometime later Dick is discharged, falls ill, and is stricken with a raging fever. When he comes to he finds himself surrounded by an assortment of bottles and basins and articles of linen airing by the fire—and the Marchioness in a chair beside his bed. "Yes; playing cribbage with herself at the table. There she sat, intent upon her game, coughing now and then in a subdued manner as if she feared to disturb him—shuffling the cards, cutting, dealing, playing, counting, pegging—going through all the mysteries of cribbage as if she had been in full practice from her cradle!"

Dick learns that he has been unconscious for three weeks and that the Marchioness has been taking care of him. At first he thinks that Sally Brass has sent the girl, but she tells him that she has run away and is quite proud that they have been "tizing" for her in the papers. Dick figures out that this means advertising for her return. He asks her, " 'And where do you live, Marchioness?' "

" 'Live!' cried the small servant. 'Here!' "

" 'Oh!' said Mr. Swiveller.

Before Dick left, young Kit Nubbles had been arrested for stealing five pounds which Brass found in the boy's hat. Dick is concerned about what has happened to the youth. The Marchioness tells him that Kit has been sentenced to be transported and continues with a tale of what she has heard bearing on the event—first telling him how she came to hear it:

" 'Well! Before I run away, I used to sleep in the kitchen— where we played cards, you know. Miss Sally used to keep the key of the kitchen door in her pocket, and she always come down at night to take away the candle and rake out the fire. When she had done that, she left me to go to bed in the dark, locked the door on the outside, put the key in her pocket again, and kept me locked up till she come down in the morning—very early I can tell you—and let me out. I was terrible afraid of being kept like this, because if there was a fire, I thought they might forget me and only take care of themselves, you know. So whenever I see an old rusty key anywhere, I picked it up and tried if it would fit the door, and at last I found in the dust-cellar a key that *did* fit it. . . .

" 'They kept me very short,' said the small servant. 'Oh! you can't think how short they kept me! So I used to come out at night after they'd gone to bed, and feel about in the dark for bits of biscuit, or sangwitches that you'd left in the office, or even pieces of orange-peel to put into cold water and make believe it was wine. Did you ever taste orange-peel and water? . . . If you make believe very much, it's quite nice,' said the small servant, 'but if you don't, you know, it seems as if it would bear a little more seasoning, certainly. Well, sometimes I used to come out after they'd gone to bed, and sometimes before, you know; and one or two nights before there was all that precious noise in the office—when the young man was took, I mean—I come upstairs while Mr. Brass and Miss Sally was a-sittin' at the office fire; and I'll tell you the truth, that I come to listen again.' "

The Marchioness heard the Brasses discussing how the dwarf Quilp wanted young Kit framed. Since Quilp was the best client of Sampson Brass, the attorney must do his bidding, and a plan was worked out for placing a five-pound note in the boy's hat and then having Dick, a friend of Kit's, search him after the loss was discovered so that it would be Dick's evidence that convicted Kit. After hearing the story Dick sent the Marchioness through the dark streets to get Mr. Garland, Kit's employer and mentor, who gets the conviction set aside. It is the Marchioness's story that starts the downfall of all the villains in the piece.

Before Dick gets well he is visited by a notary who tells him that an aunt has died and left him an annuity of one hundred and fifty pounds. Dick has a plan to spend it. "Mr. Swiveller recovering very slowly from his illness, and entering into the receipt of his annuity, bought for the Marchioness a handsome stock of clothes, and put her to school forthwith, in redemption of the vow he had made upon his fevered bed. After casting about for some time for a name which should be worthy of her, he decided in favour of Sophronia Sphynx, as being euphonious and genteel, and furthermore indicative of mystery. Under this title the Marchioness repaired, in tears, to the school of his selection, from which, as she soon distanced all competitors, she was removed before the lapse of many quarters to one of a higher grade. It is but bare justice to Mr. Swiveller to say that, although the expenses of her education kept him in straitened circumstances for half a dozen years, he never slackened in his zeal, and always held himself sufficiently repaid by the accounts he hears (with great gravity) of her advancement. . . .

"In a word, Mr. Swiveller kept the Marchioness at this establishment until she was, at a moderate guess, full nineteen years of age—good-looking, clever, and good-humoured; when he began to consider seriously what was to be done next. On one of his periodical visits, while he was revolving this question in his mind, the Marchioness came down to him, alone, looking more smiling and more fresh than ever. Then, it occurred to him, but not for the first time, that if she would marry him, how comfortable they might be! So Richard asked her; whatever she said, it wasn't No; and they were married in good earnest that day week."

In the same novel the servant girl Barbara plays a less prominent role. She has little to do with the story itself although in the end of it she marries one of the principal youthful characters, Kit Nubbles. Kit is about fifteen when he first meets Barbara on going to work for the Garlands, where the girl also works, and Barbara may be somewhat younger. At the time Kit is very much in love with Little Nell.

When Kit has been in the Garlands' employ for three months, he and Barbara receive their quarter's wages. Something of a ceremony is made of this, with the mothers of both children present, dressed in their finest. The two families plan a celebration starting with tea in Mrs. Nubbles' home, then attendance at Astleys', a combination circus and variety show, and finally an oyster supper at which Kit will, for the first time in his young life, play host. As they walk to the theater Kit and Barbara lead with the boy's toddling brother Jacob. The mothers follow behind, Mrs. Nubbles carrying the baby. "A state of things which occasioned the two mothers, who walked behind, to declare that they looked quite family folks, and caused Barbara to blush and say, 'Now don't, mother!' But Kit said she had no call to mind what they said and indeed she need not have had, if she had known how very far from Kit's thoughts any love-making was. Poor Barbara!"

After the play, fishing for information about the girl who was first in Kit's affections, Barbara asks whether Little Nell was as handsome as the lady who jumped over the ribbons.

" 'As handsome as *her?*' said Kit. 'Double as handsome.'

" 'Oh! Christopher! I'm sure she was the beautifullest creature ever was,' said Barbara.

" 'Nonsense!' returned Kit. 'She was well enough, I don't deny that; but think how she was dressed and painted, and what a difference that made. Why *you* are a good deal better-looking than her, Barbara.'

" 'Oh, Christopher!' said Barbara, looking down.

" 'You are, any day,' said Kit—'and so's your mother.'
"Poor Barbara!"

At supper Kit plays the man-about-town with a demeanor
that belies his tender years, although it is evident that he is
somewhat uncertain as to how his adult stance will be re-
received by the minions of the establishment. He walks into
the oyster shop "as bold as if he lived there," and leads his
party into a box, "a private box, fitted up with red curtains,
white table cloth, and cruet-stand complete." He orders a
fierce gentleman with whiskers who calls him "sir" to bring
"three dozen of the largest oysters, and look sharp about it!"
He is somewhat surprised when the fierce gentleman obeys
and when he returns becomes more bold and orders a pot of
beer; "and the gentleman, instead of replying, 'Sir, did you
address that language to me?' only said, 'Pot o' beer, sir? Yes,
sir,' and went off and fetched it. . . .

"Then they fell to work upon the supper in earnest; and
there was Barbara, that foolish Barbara, declaring that she
could not eat more than two, and wanting more pressing than
you would believe before she would eat four: though her
mother and Kit's mother made up for it pretty well, and ate
and laughed and enjoyed themselves so thoroughly that it did
Kit good to see them, and made him laugh and eat likewise
from strong sympathy. But the greatest miracle of the night
was little Jacob, who ate oysters as if he had been born and
bred to the business—sprinkled the pepper and the vinegar
with a discretion beyond his years—and afterwards built a
grotto on the table with the shells. There was the baby too,
who had never closed an eye all night, but had sat as good as
gold, trying to force a large orange into his mouth, and gaz-
ing intently at the lights in the chandelier—there he was, sitting up in his mother's lap, staring at the gas without winking,

and making indentations in his soft visage with an oyster-shell, to that degree that a heart of iron must have loved him! In short, there never was a more successful supper."

Barbara appears no more until the next to the last page of the book when Kit, whose love for Nell did not long survive her demise, marries his fellow servant. "And the best of it was, he married so soon that little Jacob was an uncle, before the calves of his legs, already mentioned in this history, had even been encased in broadcloth pantaloons."

One of Dickens' strangest incidental juvenile characters is Jenny Wren in *Our Mutual Friend*. Her name is really Fanny Cleaver, but she prefers to call herself Jenny Wren. She is presumably twelve or thriteen years old and is either deformed or the victim of some kind of paralytic disease. In any event she has a bad back and her legs are, in her own words, "queer." She plays no particular part in the story line of the novel but is memorable for some of her speeches, which illustrate Dickens' ability to portray the mental proc-esses and fancies of a twelve-year-old who, for physical rea-sons, is isolated from the world of childhood. Jenny keeps house for, and manages, a drunken father. She is first intro-duced when Charley Hexam and Bradley Headstone come to call on Charley's sister, another adolescent who lodges with Jenny.

"The boy knocked at a door, and the door promptly opened with a spring and a click. A parlor door within a small entry stood open, and disclosed a child—a dwarf—a girl—a something—sitting on a little low old-fashioned arm-chair, which had a kind of little working-bench before it.

" 'I can't get up,' said the child, 'because my back's bad, and my legs are queer. But I'm the person of the house.'

" 'Who else is at home?' asked Charley Hexam, staring.

" 'Nobody's at home at present,' returned the child, with a glib assertion of her dignity, 'except the person of the house. What did you want, young man?'

" 'I wanted to see my sister.'

" 'Many young men have sisters,' returned the child. 'Give me your name, young man.'

"The queer little figure, and the queer but not ugly little face, with its bright grey eyes, were so sharp, that the sharpness of the manner seemed unavoidable. As if, being turned out of that mould, it must be sharp."

Jenny is cutting and pasting scraps of cardboard, silk, velvet, and ribbon very industriously as she talks, and Headstone is fascinated by what she is doing and asks about her occupation. Jenny makes him guess and when he fails she tells him, " 'I'm a Doll's Dressmaker.' "

" 'I hope it's a good business?'

"The person of the house shrugs her shoulders and shakes her head. 'No, poorly paid. And I'm often so pressed for time! I had a doll married, last week, and was obliged to work all night. And it's not good for me, on account of my back being so bad and my legs so queer.'

"They looked at the little creature with a wonder that did not diminish, and the schoolmaster said: 'I am sorry your fine ladies are so inconsiderate.'

" 'It's the way with them,' said the person of the house, shrugging her shoulders again. 'And they take no care of their clothes, and they never keep to the same fashions a month. I work for a doll with three daughters. Bless you, she's enough to ruin her husband!'

"The person of the house gave a weird little laugh here, and gave them another look out of the corners of her eyes. She had an elfin chin that was capable of great expression, and whenever she gave this look she hitched this chin up. As if her eyes and her chin worked together on the same wires.

" 'Are you always as busy as you are now?'

" 'Busier. I'm slack just now. I finished a large mourning order the day before yesterday. Doll I work for lost a canary bird.' "

Headstone asks her whether she is alone all day and whether any of the neighboring children ——. At the word children the little dressmaker delivers a tirade against her contemporaries, spawned by the difference between herself and normal children. She screams: " 'Don't talk of children. I can't bear children. *I* know their tricks and their manners. . . . Always running about and screeching, always playing and fighting, always skip-skip-skipping on the pavement and chalking it for their games! Oh! *I* know their tricks and their manners!' Shaking the little fist as before. 'And that's not all. Ever so often calling names in through a person's keyhole, and imitating a person's back and legs. Oh! *I* know their tricks and their manners. And I'll tell you what I'd do to punish them. There's doors under the church in the Square—black doors, leading into black vaults. Well! I'd open one of those doors, and I'd cram 'em all in, and then I'd lock the door and through the keyhole I'd blow in pepper.'

" 'What would be the good of blowing in pepper?' asked Charley Hexam.

" 'To set 'em sneezing,' said the person of the house, 'and make their eyes water. And when they were all sneezing and inflamed, I'd mock 'em through the keyhole. Just as they, with their tricks and their manners, mock a person through a person's keyhole!' "

A couple of Jenny's speeches are worth quoting because of their illustration of Dickens' understanding of juvenile imagery. The child said that she frequently smelled flowers although " 'this is not a very flowery neighborhood. I have seen very few flowers indeed in my life.' " And she heard birds sing.

"There was something in the face and action for the moment quite inspired and beautiful. Then the chin dropped musingly upon the hand again.

" 'I dare say my birds sing better than other birds, and my flowers smell better than other flowers. For when I was a little child,' in a tone as though it were ages ago, 'the children that I used to see early in the morning were very different from any others that I ever saw. They were not like me; they were not chilled, anxious, ragged, or beaten; they were never in pain. They were not like the children of the neighbors; they never made me tremble all over by setting up shrill noises, and they never mocked me. Such numbers of them too! All in white dresses, and with something shining on the borders, and on their heads, that I have never been able to imitate with my work, though I know it so well. They used to come down in long bright slanting rows, and say all to-together, "Who is this in pain! Who is this in pain!" When I told them who it was, they answered, "Come and play with us!" When I said "I never play! I can't play!" they swept about me and took me up, and made me light. Then it was all delicious ease and rest till they laid me down, and said, all together, "Have patience, and we will come again." Whenever they came back, I used to know they were coming before I saw the long bright rows, by hearing them ask, all together a long way off, "Who is this in pain! Who is this in pain!" And I used to cry out, "O my blessed children, it's poor me. Have pity on me. Take me up and make me light!" ' "

On another occasion she is on a housetop on a hill from which, she says, " 'you see the clouds rushing on above the narrow streets, not minding them, and you see the golden arrows pointing at the mountains in the sky from which the wind comes, and you feel as if you were dead.' "

"The little creature looked above her, holding up her slight transparent hand.

" 'How do you feel when you are dead?' asked Fledgeby, much perplexed.

" 'Oh, so tranquil!' cried the little creature, smiling. 'Oh, so peaceful and so thankful! And you hear the people who are alive, crying and working, and calling to one another down in the close dark streets, and you seem to pity them so! And such a chain has fallen from you, and such a strange good sorrowful happiness comes upon you!' "

One of Dickens' most forceful expositions of a child thoroughly doomed by the society of the time was that of Jo the street sweeper in *Bleak House*. Jo was utterly neglected physically, mentally, and spiritually by all of the agencies of that society. When the boy is ill, one character in the book asks: "Is it not a horrible reflection that if this wretched creature were a convicted prisoner, his hospital would be wide open to him." Instead Jo dies of fever in the back of a shooting gallery. Dickens' characterization of this waif of the slums was based on an actual boy who met a similar, unattended death and whose case attracted wide attention.

Jo is first introduced at an inquest into the death of a legal copy clerk who was the only person who seemed to have befriended him. "Here he is, very muddy, very hoarse, very ragged. Now, boy!—But stop a minute. Caution. This boy must be put through a few preliminary paces.

"Name, Jo. Nothing else that he knows on. Don't know

that everybody has two names. Never heard of sich a think. Don't know that Jo is short for a longer name. Thinks it long enough for *him*. *He* don't find no fault with it. Spell it? No. *He* can't spell it. No father, no mother, no friends. Never been to school. What's home? Knows a broom's a broom, and knows it's wicked to tell a lie. Don't recollect who told him about the broom, or about the lie, but knows both. Can't exactly say what'll be done to him arter he's dead if he tells a lie to the gen'l'men here, but believes it'll be something wery bad to punish him, and serve him right—and so he'll tell the truth."

The coroner is irate that such a witness has even been brought before him. His evidence certainly cannot be heard. " 'Out of the question,' says the coroner. 'You have heard the boy. "Can't exactly say" won't do, you know. We can't take *that*, in a Court of Justice, gentlemen. It's terrible depravity. Put the boy aside.' "

Dickens comments, with insight as well as pity, on the meaning of life to such boys as Jo. "It must be a strange state to be like Jo! To shuffle through the streets, unfamiliar with the shapes, and in utter darkness as to the meaning of those mysterious symbols, so abundant over the shops, and at the corners of streets, and on the doors, and in the windows! To see people read, and to see people write, and to see the postmen deliver letters, and not to have the least idea of all that language—to be, to every scrap of it, stone blind and dumb! It must be very puzzling to see the good company going to the churches on Sundays, with their books in their hands, and to think (for perhaps Jo *does* think, at odd times) what does it all mean, and if it means anything to anybody, how comes it that it means nothing to Me? To be hustled, and jostled, and moved on; and really to feel that it would appear to be

perfectly true that I have no business, here, or there, or anywhere; and yet to be perplexed by the consideration that I
am here somehow, too, and everybody overlooked me until
I became the creature that I am! It must be a strange state,
not merely to be told that I am scarcely human (as in the
case of my offering myself for a witness), but to feel it of
my own knowledge all my life! To see the horses, dogs, and
cattle, go by me, and to know that in ignorance I belong to
them, and not to the superior beings in my shape, whose
delicacy I offend! Jo's ideas of a Criminal Trial, or a Judge,
or a Bishop, or a Government, or that inestimable jewel to
him (if he only knew it), the Constitution, should be strange!
His whole material and immaterial life is wonderfully strange;
his death, the strangest thing of all."

Dickens uses Jo to express his views on some aspects of religion. At the time there was great zeal for foreign missions,
for bringing the Word to the unenlightened heathen. Dickens believed that much of this spiritual charity could have
been better spent at home. "Jo . . . sits down to breakfast on
the doorstep of the Society for the Propagation of the Gospel
in Foreign Parts, and gives it a brush when he has finished, as
an acknowledgment of the accommodation. He admires the
size of the edifice, and wonders what it's all about. He has no
idea, poor wretch, of the spiritual destitution of a coral reef
in the Pacific, or what it costs to look up the precious souls
among the coconuts and bread-fruit."

In the interest of the times Jo was not a fit subject for the
good works of religious institutions. He was not a glamorous
or dramatic primitive; merely a small, dirty creature whom it
was more comfortable to ignore. Wrote Dickens: "Jo . . . is
not softened by distance and unfamiliarity; he is not a genuine foreign-grown savage; he is the ordinary home-made

article. Dirty, ugly, disagreeable to all the senses, in body a common creature of the common streets, only in soul a heathen. Homely filth begrimes him, homely parasites devour him, homely sores are in him, homely rags are on him: native ignorance, the growth of English soil and climate, sinks his immortal nature lower than the beasts that perish. Stand forth, Jo, in uncompromising colour! From the sole of thy foot to the crown of thy head, there is nothing interesting about thee."

The whole meaning of religion has never been presented in such a way that Jo can understand it. Just before his death, an adult character who has befriended the boy asks:

" 'Jo! Did you ever know a prayer?'

" 'Never knowd nothink, sir.'

" 'Not so much as one short prayer?'

" 'No, sir. Nothink at all. Mr. Chadbands he wos a-prayin' wunst at Mr. Sangsby's and I heerd him, but he sounded as if he wos a-speakin' to hisself, and not to me. He prayed a lot, but I couldn't make out nothink of it. Different times, there was other gen'l'men come down to Tom-all-Alone's [the slum where Jo lived] a-prayin', but they all mostly sed as the t'other wuns prayed wrong, and all mostly sounded to be a-talkin' to theirselves, or a-passin' blame on t'others, and not a-talkin' to us. We never knowd nothink. I never knowd what it wos all about.' ...

" 'Jo, can you say what I say?'

" 'I'll say anythink as you say, sir, for I knows it's good.'

" 'OUR FATHER.'

" 'Our Father!—yes, that's wery good, sir.'

" 'WHICH ART IN HEAVEN.'

" 'Art in Heaven—is the light a-comin', sir?'

" 'It is close at hand. HALLOWED BE THY NAME!'

" 'Hallowed be—thy—'

"The light is come upon the dark benighted way. Dead! Dead, Your Majesty. Dead, my lords and gentlemen. Dead, Right Reverends and Wrong Reverends of every order. Dead, men and women, born with Heavenly compassion in your hearts. And dying thus around us every day."

In several instances Dickens uses his juvenile characters to express his opposition to the Calvanistic doctrine which held that children were born sinful and must be beaten into a semblance of grace. Of the "gloomy taint" of the Murd-stone's "austere and wrathful" religion he has David Copper-field say: "As to any recreation with other children my age, I had very little of that; for the gloomy theology of the Murdstones made all children out to be a swarm of vipers (though there *was* a child once set in the midst of the disciples) and held that they contaminated one another. The natural result of this treatment . . . was to make me sullen, dull, and dogged."

Dickens also derided the practice of worship as it was conducted in the churches and by strict parents as being meaningless and frightening to a child. In *Little Dorrit* a church bell reminds Arthur Clennam of the Sundays of his youth. "Its sound had revived a long train of miserable Sundays, and the procession would not stop with the bell, but continued to march on. 'Heaven forgive me,' said he, 'and those who trained me. How I have hated this day!'

"There was the dreary Sunday of his childhood, when he sat with his hands before him, scared out of his senses by a horrible tract which commenced business with the poor child by asking him in its title, why he was going to Perdition?—a piece of curiosity that he really in a frock and drawers was not in a condition to satisfy—and which, for the further attraction of his infant mind, had a parenthesis in every other line with some such hiccupping reference as 2Ep. Thess, c.iii.v 6&7. There was the sleepy Sunday of his boyhood, when, like a military deserter, he was marched to chapel by a picquet of teachers three times a day, morally handcuffed to another boy; and when he would willingly have bartered two meals of indigestible sermon for another ounce or two of inferior mutton at his scanty dinner in the flesh. There was the interminable Sunday of his nonage, when his mother, stern of face and unrelenting of heart, would sit all day behind a bible—bound like her own construction of it in the hardest, barest, and straitest boards, with one dinted ornament on the cover like the drag of a chain, and a wrathful sprinkling of red upon the edges of the leaves—as if it, of all books! were a fortification against sweetness of temper, natural affection, and gentle intercourse."

The theme of a child's baffled misunderstanding of religion and of the relation between the living and the dead is a background for the introduction of Pip in *Great Expectations*. Pip is an orphan and his exact age is not given but it is presumably about eight when he is introduced on the first page of the novel, reminiscing about his deceased parents and expressing his conception of their appearance as gained from the legends on their tombstones:

"The shape of the letters on my father's gave me an odd idea that he was a square, stout, dark man, with curly black hair. From the character and turn of the inscription, 'Also Georgiana Wife of the Above,' I drew a childish conclusion that my mother was freckled and sickly. To five little stone lozenges, each about a foot and a half long, which were arranged in a neat row beside their grave, and were sacred to the memory of five little brothers of mine—who gave up try-

ing to get a living exceedingly early in that universal struggle
—I am indebted for a belief I religiously entertained that they
had all been born on their backs with their hands in their
trousers pockets, and had never taken them out in this state
of existence. . . . I read 'Wife of the Above' as a complimentary reference to my father's exaltation to a better world;
and if any one of my deceased relations had been referred to
as 'Below,' I have no doubt I should have formed the worst
opinions of that member of the family. Neither were my no-
tions of the theological positions to which my Catechism
bound me at all accurate; for I have a lively remembrance
that I supposed my declaration that I was to 'walk in the
same all the days of my life,' laid me under an obligation always to go through the village from our house in one particular direction, and never to vary it by turning down by the
wheelwright's or up by the mill."

Great Expectations is principally a biography of Pip, during most of which he is an adult, and the grown-up Pip is the
narrator of the story. His youthful years occupy about the
first third of the novel. Although this child is brought up
with less than kindness and parental affection, he is not one
of Dickens' pathetic heroes, buffeted by the slings and arrows
of a cruel world. He is neither poverty-stricken, ill, nor
completely rejected. His boyhood is that of a small-town
boy with such a youth's problems; his adolescence, of which
Dickens makes very little, is one of affluence. In his younger
years the author discloses much of his own understanding of
childish views on morality, fear, fantasy, and sensitiveness.

Pip is brought up by his much older sister, Georgiana Gargery, and her husband Joe, an illiterate blacksmith. Joe is a
good-natured ally of Pip's, but the sister is a thorough shrew.
She had, recalled Pip, "established a great reputation with

herself and the neighbors because she had brought me up 'by hand.' Having at that time to find out for myself what the expression meant, and knowing her to have a hard and heavy hand, and to be much in the habit of laying it upon her husband, as well as upon me, I supposed that Joe Gargery and I were both brought up by hand." The boy summarizes the attitude of his surrogate mother by saying: "I think my sister must have had some general idea that I was a young offender whom an Accoucheur Policeman had taken up (on my birthday) and delivered over to her, to be dealt with according to the outraged majesty of the law. I was always treated as if I had insisted on being born in opposition to the dictates of reason, religion, and morality, and against the dissuading arguments of my best friends."

Pip's first fearsome experience is an encounter with an escaped convict, Magwich, on Christmas Eve in a graveyard. "A fearful man, all in coarse grey, with a great iron on his leg. A man with no hat, and with broken shoes, and with an old rag tied round his head. A man who had been soaked in water, and smothered in mud, and lamed by stones, and cut by flints, and stung by nettles, and torn by briars; who limped and shivered, and glared and growled, and whose teeth chattered in his head as he seized me by the chin." The fearsome man tells Pip that he must bring him food and a file and warns him that if he does not, or tells anybody about it, "I'll have your heart and liver out." Worse, he will turn him over to a mysterious young man who is hiding with him who "has a secret way peculiar to himself, of getting at a boy, and at his heart, and at his liver." Terror stricken, Pip promises to bring the required materials and at dawn the next morning steals various edibles from the pantry and a file from Joe's forge, which he takes to the misty graveyard.

Later in the morning Pip goes to church with Joe and is
beset by fears of his wickedness. "What I suffered outside,
was nothing to what I underwent within. The terrors that
had assailed me whenever Mrs. Joe had gone near the pantry,
or out of the room, were only to be equalled by the remorse
with which my mind dwelt on what my hands had done.
Under the weight of my wicked secret, I pondered whether
the Church would be powerful enough to shield me from the
vengeance of the terrible young man, if I divulged to that
establishment. I conceived the idea that the time when the
banns were read and when the clergyman said, 'Ye are now
to declare it!' would be the time for me to rise and propose
a private conference in the vestry. I am far from being sure
that I might not have astonished our small congregation by
resorting to this extreme measure, but for its being Christmas
Day and no Sunday."

When his sister goes to the pantry to get a pork pie which
he had stolen for Magwich, Pip recalls: "I have never been
absolutely certain whether I uttered a shrill yell of terror,
merely in spirit, or in the bodily hearing of the company. I
felt that I could bear no more, and that I must run away. I
released the leg of the table, and ran for my life." At the door
he meets a file of soldiers who distract the diners from the
missing pie. The soldiers soon capture Magwich, who pro-
tects Pip by claiming that he broke into the house and stole
the food and file.

But even though he is free from detection, Pip is not easy
in his mind. The adult Pip recalls: "Few people know what
secrecy there is in the young, under terror. No matter how
unreasonable the terror, so that it be terror." It is not only
fear that holds Pip back from confession, but the effect
that this will have on the relation of others toward him, par-

ticularly Joe. "I do not recall that I felt any tenderness of conscience in reference to Mrs. Joe, when the fear of being found out was lifted off me. But I loved Joe—perhaps for no better reason in those early days than because the dear fellow let me love him—and, as to him, my inner self was not so easily composed. It was much upon my mind (particularly when I first saw him looking about for his file) that I ought to tell Joe the whole truth. Yet I did not, and for the reason that I mistrusted that if I did, he would think me worse than I was. The fear of losing Joe's confidence, and of thenceforth sitting in the chimney corner at night staring drearily at my forever lost companion and friend, tied up my tongue."

At this time Pip went to that ludicrous school conducted by Mr. Wopsle's great-aunt, which has previously been described, where he "struggled through the alphabet as if it had been a bramble bush, getting considerably worried and scratched by every letter." The great-aunt was assisted by Biddy, a girl slightly older than Pip, who later came to work for the Gargerys as one of Dickens' innumerable servant girls. Biddy . . . "was an orphan like myself; like me, too, had been brought up by hand. She was most noticeable, I thought, in respect of her extremities; for her hair always wanted brushing, her hands always wanted washing, and her shoes always wanted mending and pulling up at the heel. This description must be received with a week-day limitation. On Sundays she went to church elaborated."

The begininng of a change in Pip's life takes place when his uncle, Mr. Pumblechook, announces that he has been instructed by a Miss Havisham to bring Pip to play there. Miss Havisham is known far and wide as an eccentric old woman, presumably very wealthy, who lives in a large, desolate house on the edge of town. Here he is admitted by Estella, an im-

perious young miss who calls him *boy*, "with carelessness that
was far from complimentary; she was of about my own age.
She seemed much older than I, of course, being a girl, and
beautiful and self-possessed; and she was as scornful of me as
if she had been one-and-twenty, and a queen."

Estella is the heroine of the story, if she can be called a
heroine; she is a far cry from the saintly young ladies who
were Dickens' favorites for this position. It is later explained
that the pride and haughtiness that characterize her for much
of the book are not entirely her fault. She had been adopted
at the age of three by Miss Havisham, who had been a beautiful heiress in her youth, but had literally been left at the
altar by a young man who had courted her only to borrow
money. Embittered toward all mankind, Miss Havisham had
shut herself into her magnificent home, covered the windows,
and stopped the clocks to renounce the world. Much later
she had adopted Estella at the age of three and raised her, in
the then desolate mansion, educating her to steel her heart
against all tenderness but to lead young men on to love her,
that she might break their hearts.

Miss Havisham now has the whim that a boy should come
and play with Estella—perhaps, at this tender age, to start her
training as a heartbreaker. She orders the children to play
cards. "With this boy!" cries the girl. "Why, he is a common labouring-boy . . . And what coarse hands he has! And
what thick boots!" When Pip leaves, the girl is instructed to
give him some food and she places bread and meat and a mug
of beer on the stones of the yard for him, "as if I was a dog
in disgrace. I was so humiliated, hurt, spurned, offended, angry, sorry—I cannot hit upon the right name for the smart—
God knows what its name was—that tears started to my eyes.
The moment they sprang there, the girl looked at me with a

quick delight in having been the cause of them. This gave me power to keep them back and to look at her: so, she gave me a contemptuous look—but with a sense, I thought, of having made too sure that I was so wounded—and left me."

It is here that Dickens makes the point about the sensitiveness of children, noted earlier in this volume. Pip recalls: "My sister's bringing me up had made me sensitive. In the little world in which children have their existence, whosoever brings them up, there is nothing so finely perceived and so finely felt, as injustice. It may be only small injustice that the child can be exposed to; but the child is small, and its world is small, and its rocking-horse stands as many hands high, according to scale, as a big-boned Irish hunter. Within myself, I had sustained, from my babyhood, a perpetual conflict with injustice. I had known, from the time when I could speak, that my sister, in her capricious and violent coercion, was unjust to me. I had cherished a profound conviction that her bringing me up by hand gave her no right to bring me up by jerks. Through all my punishments, disgraces, fasts, and vigils, and other penitential performances, I had nursed this assurance; and to my communing so much with it, in a solitary and unprotected way, I in great part refer the fact that I was morally timid and very sensitive."

When Pip gets home there is great curiosity about his visit with Miss Havisham, and another childish characteristic is disclosed in Pip. If he truthfully tells what happened, adults will not understand him. "If a dread of not being understood be hidden in the breasts of other young people to anything like the extent to which it used to be hidden in mine—which I consider probable, as I have no particular reason to suspect myself of having been a monstrosity—it is the key to many reservations."

Pip tries not to say anything, but the terrible Uncle Pumblechook cross-examines him until he is drawn into inventing a series of fantastic adventures. Soon the pleasure of exercising his imagination and astounding his tormentors with his nonsense leads him to further embroider his tale. Miss Havisham, he says, was sitting in a black velvet coach in a candle-lit room. " 'And Miss Estella—that's her niece, I think—handed her in cake and wine at the coach-window, on a gold plate. And we all had cake and wine on gold plates. And I got up behind the coach to eat mine, because she told me to.'

" 'Was anybody else there?' asked Mr. Pumblechook.

" 'Four dogs,' said I.

" 'Large or small?'

" 'Immense,' said I. 'And they fought for veal-cutlets out of a silver basket.'

"Mr. Pumblechook and Mrs. Joe stared at one another again, in utter amazement. I was perfectly frantic—a reckless witness under the torture—and would have told them anything. . . .

" 'What did you play at, boy?'

" 'We played with flags,' I said.

" 'Flags!' echoed my sister.

" 'Yes,' said I. 'Estella waved a blue flag, and I waved a red one, and Miss Havisham waved one sprinkled all over with little gold stars, out at the coach-window. And then we all waved our swords and hurrahed.' "

The Havisham visit marks the beginning of Pip becoming the snob that he is throughout much of the novel. Estella's attitude toward him makes him aware of the difference between an apprentice to a blacksmith with coarse hands and thick boots and a budding gentleman of culture, and he be-

lieves that he will never be satisfied until he has attained the
latter stature, impossible as its attainment may seem. The
new feeling makes him most unhappy. "It is a most miserable
thing to feel ashamed of home. There may be black ingrati-
tude in the thing, and the punishment may be retributive and
well deserved; but, that it is a miserable thing, I can testify."

On a long walk he discusses his problem at length with the
sensible Biddy. Biddy could well be the subject of his affections rather than Estella. But the contempt of the beautiful
girl has confused him and aroused longings that cannot be
denied. On the one hand he thinks that he would be happier
in the simple life at the forge with his close companion Joe.
"If I could have settled down and been but half as fond of
the forge as I was when I was little, I know it would have
been much better for me. You and I and Joe would have
wanted nothing then, and Joe and I would perhaps have gone
partners." He says to Biddy: "If only I could get myself to
fall in love with you."

"But you never will, you see," said Biddy. . . .

"It was clear that Biddy was immeasurably better than
Estella, and that the plain honest working life to which I was
born had nothing in it to be ashamed of, but offered me sufficient means of self-respect and happiness . . . when all in a
moment some confounding remembrance of the Havisham
days would fall upon me, like a destructive missile, and scatter
my wits again. Scattered wits take a long time picking up;
and often, before I had got them well together, they would
be dispersed in all directions by one stray thought."

Pip's future is decided, one day in his early teens, when a
lawyer calls to say that a benefactor who must remain anonymous has assigned a handsome property to Pip on condition

"that he be immediately removed from his present sphere of life, and from this place, and be brought up as a gentleman— in a word, as a young fellow of great expectations." Thus the title of the book. He is outfitted in fine clothes by Trabb, the local tailor, and sent to London to a tutor. Dickens makes little of Pip's later adolescence, merely presenting him rather impersonally as a junior playboy. One delightful incident contrasting the self-consciousness and lack of assurance that really underlay the surface poise of the youthful man-about-town with the simple deviltry of a younger boy takes place when Pip goes home and struts the streets of the town in his London finery. He relates:

"My position was a distinguished one, and I was not at all dissatisfied with it, until Fate threw me in the way of that unlimited miscreant, Trabb's boy. . . . I beheld Trabb's boy approaching, lashing himself with an empty blue bag. Deeming that a serene and unconscious contemplation of him would best beseem me, and would be most likely to quell his evil mind, I advanced with that expression of countenance, and was rather congratulating myself on my success, when suddenly the knees of Trabb's boy smote together, his hair uprose, his cap fell off, he trembled violently in every limb, staggered out into the road, and crying to the populace, 'Hold me! I'm so frightened!' feigned to be in a paroxysm of terror and contrition, occasioned by the dignity of my appearance. . . .

"I had not got as much further down the street as the post office when I again beheld Trabb's boy shooting round by a back way. This time, he was entirely changed. He wore the blue bag in the manner of my great-coat, and was strutting along the pavement towards me on the opposite side of the street, attended by a company of delighted young friends to whom he from time to time exclaimed, with a wave of his hand, 'Don't know yah!' Words cannot state the amount of aggravation and injury wreaked upon me by Trabb's boy, when, passing abreast of me, he pulled up his shirt-collar, twined his sidehair, stuck an arm akimbo, and smirked extravagantly by, wriggling his elbows and body, and drawling to his attendants 'Don't know yah, don't know yah, pon my soul, don't know yah!' The disgrace attendant on his immediately afterwards taking to crowing and pursuing me across the bridge with crows, as from an exceedingly dejected fowl who had known me when I was a blacksmith, culminated the disgrace with which I left the town, and was, so to speak, ejected by it into the open country."

This is the end of the story of the juvenile Pip. When he reaches his majority he comes into the principal of his handsome estate. He has always assumed that Miss Havisham was his benefactor, but one night there comes to his rooms a bedraggled, bewhiskered man whom he recognizes as Magwich, the criminal whom he had met in the churchyard as a youth. It transpires that Magwich has settled the estate on him and that he is Estella's father. The proud beauty has been married by her foster mother to an ill-tempered young man who has nothing to recommend him except money and a ridiculous role of addlepated predecessors. After several extremely unhappy years she leaves her husband, who subsequently dies. Meanwhile Pip's sister dies and he passes through a serious illness, during which he sees the error of his ways and is reunited with Joe. At the end of the book he meets the widowed Estella where they had first met. "I took her hand in mine, and we went out of the ruined place; and as the morn-

ing mists had risen long ago, when I first left the forge, so the
evening mists were rising now; and in all the broad expanse
of tranquil light they showed to me, I saw the shadow of no
parting from her."

CHAPTER
VII

SOME HAPPIER CHILDREN

There are some happy children in Dickens' novels, although
none play principal, and few fill important subordinate, roles
in the stories. In the main they are incidental youngsters
found in batches as the offspring of families in which there is
parental warmth and affection. Dickens was a firm believer
in the home and the hearth and parental love as the root of all
juvenile happiness and on occasion "threw in" a family in
which such an atmosphere prevailed.

One such is the Toodle family in *Dombey and Son*. Mrs.
Toodle (whom Mr. Dombey dubbed Richards for no apparent reason) is Paul's nurse immediately after his mother's
death. Her husband is a locomotive stoker. The Toodles are
brought *en masse* to be viewed by Mr. Dombey before
Richards is hired. The family includes "a plump, rosy-
cheeked, wholesome apple-faced young woman, with an infant in her arms; a younger woman not so plump, but apple-
faced also, who led a plump and apple-faced child in each

hand; another plump and also apple-faced boy who walked by himself; and finally, a plump and apple-faced man, who carried in his arms another plump and apple-faced boy, whom he stood down on the floor, and admonished, in a husky whisper, to 'kitch hold of' his brother Johnny."

After Paul's christening Mrs. Toodle—Polly—sneaks off with Susan Nipper and Florence to visit her children, whom her sister, the second apple-cheeked young woman at the presentation, is taking care of. The sister avers that the children: 'Will go half wild to see you, Polly, that they will.'

"That they did, if one might judge from the noise they made, and the way in which they dashed at Polly and dragged her to a low chair in the chimney corner, where her own honest apple-face became immediately the centre of a bunch of smaller pippins, all laying their rosy cheeks close to it, and all evidently the growth of the same tree. As to Polly, she was full as noisy and vehement as the children; and it was not until she was quite out of breath, and her hair was hanging all about her flushed face, and her new christening attire was very much dishevelled, that any pause took place in the confusion. Even then, the smallest Toodle but one remained in her lap holding on tight with both arms round her neck; while the smallest Toodle but two mounted on the back of the chair, and made desperate efforts, with one leg in the air, to kiss her round the corner."

The family is portrayed later in the book gathered round their father as he has tea while "conveying the two young Toodles on his knees to Birmingham by special engine." He hands out tidbits to the expectant circle of his offspring, "by holding out great wedges of bread-and-butter, to be bitten at by the family in lawful succession, and by serving out small doses of tea in like manner with a spoon; which snacks had such a relish in the mouths of these young Toodles that, after partaking of the same, they performed private dances of ecstasy among themselves, and stood on one leg a-piece and hopped, and indulged in other saltatory tokens of gladness."

Another harmonious family aggregation is incidently introduced into *Nicholas Nickleby* in the persons of the Kenwigs. Mr. Kenwigs is a turner in ivory, and a person of "some consideration." Mrs. Kenwigs is "quite a lady in her manners, and of a very genteel family, having an uncle who collected a water-rate; besides which distinction, the two eldest of her little girls went twice a week to a dancing school in the neighbourhood, and had flaxen hair, tied with blue ribands, hanging in luxuriant pigtails down their backs; and wore little white trousers with frills round the ancles—for all of which reasons, and many more equally valid but too numerous to mention, Mrs. Kenwigs was considered a very desirable person to know, and was the constant theme of all the gossips in the street, and even three or four doors round the corner at both ends."

At a family dinner to honor Uncle Lillyvick, the water-rent collector, the guest of honor is seated in an armchair by the fire, "the four little Kenwigses disposed on a small form in front of the company with their flaxen tails towards them, and their faces to the fire; an arrangement which was no sooner perfected, than Mrs. Kenwigs was overpowered by the feelings of a mother, and fell upon the left shoulder of Mr. Kenwigs dissolved in tears.

" 'They are so beautiful!' said Mrs. Kenwigs, sobbing.

" 'Oh, dear,' said all the ladies, 'so they are! It's very natural you should feel proud of that; but don't give way, don't.' " 'I cannot help it, and it don't signify,' sobbed Mrs.

Kenwigs. 'Oh! they're too beautiful to live, much too beautiful!'

"On hearing this alarming presentiment of their being doomed to an early death in the flower of their infancy, all four little girls raised a hideous cry, and burying their heads in their mother's lap simultaneously, screamed until the eight flaxen tails vibrated again; Mrs. Kenwigs meanwhile clasping them alternately to her bosom."

The most amusing harmonious family is that of the Crummles, also in *Nicholas Nickleby*. When Nicholas leaves Dotheboys Hall with Smike he heads toward Portsmouth, planning to go to sea as a last resort. On the way he stops at an inn and is introduced to a dining room where, the proprietor tells him, he might eat with another gentleman. At the upper end of the room, when he enters it, "were a couple of boys, one of them very tall and the other very short, both dressed as sailors—or at least as theatrical sailors, with belts, buckles, pigtails, and pistols complete—fighting what is called in play-bills a terrific combat, with two of those short broadswords with basket hilts which are commonly used at our minor theaters. The short boy had gained a great advantage over the tall boy, who was reduced to mortal strait, and both were overlooked by a large heavy man, perched against the corner of a table, who emphatically adjured them to strike a little more fire out of the swords, and they couldn't fail to bring the house down, on the very first night."

The heavy man is Mr. Crummles, the boys his two sons. The Crummles are a theatrical family of which all members get into the act. The father is immediately taken with Smike, of whom he says, "without a pad upon his body, and hardly a touch of paint upon his face, he'd make such an actor for the starved business as was never seen in this country. . . . I never saw a young fellow so regularly cut out for that line, since I've been in the profession. And I played the heavy children when I was eighteen months old."

Nicholas and Smike join Mr. Crummles' troupe, the latter to play the Apothecary in *Romeo and Juliet* and the former to write playbills, translate plays, and appear in minor roles. They proceed toward Portsmouth behind a pony who is also part of the troupe and comes from a distinguished show-business family. His mother "ate apple-pie at a circus for upwards of fourteen years, fired pistols, and went to bed in a nightcap; and, in short, took the low comedy entirely." His father had been a dancer but, said Crummles, "he was rather a low sort of pony. The fact is, he had been originally jobbed out by the day, and he never quite got over his old habits. He was clever in melodrama too, but too broad—too broad. When the mother died, he took the port-wine business.'

" 'The port-wine business!' cried Nicholas.

" 'Drinking port wine with the clown,' said the manager; 'but he was greedy, and one night bit off the bowl of the glass, and choked himself, so his vulgarity was the death of him at last.' "

At Portsmouth the group go to the theater where Nicholas meets Mrs. Crummles and sees their daughter practice a ballet. This maiden is introduced to Nicholas as "the infant phenomenon—Miss Ninetta Crummles."

" 'Your daugher?' inquired Nicholas.

" 'My daughter—my daughter,' replied Mr. Vincent Crummles; 'the idol of every place we go into, sir. We have had complimentary letters about this girl, sir, from the nobility and gentry of almost every town in England.'

" 'I am not surprised at that,' said Nicholas; 'she must be quite a natural genius.'

" 'Quite a ——!' Mr. Crummles stopped: language was not powerful enough to describe the infant phenomenon. 'I'll tell you what, sir,' he said; 'the talent of this child is not to be imagined. She must be seen, sir—seen—to be ever so faintly appreciated.' "

Mr. Crummles proudly states that the infant phenomenon is only ten years old. Nicholas responds that this is extraordinary. "It was; for the infant phenomenon, though of short stature, had a comparatively aged countenance, and had moreover been precisely the same age—not perhaps to the full extent of the memory of the oldest inhabitant, but certainly for five good years. But she had been kept up late every night, and put upon an unlimited allowance of gin-and-water from infancy, to prevent her growing tall, and perhaps this system of training had produced in the infant phenomenon these additional phenomena."

Dickens had a rather simple formula for childhood happiness. It existed only in nature. The country was the place where children could be free to enjoy the spirit of childhood. The city corrupted them, suppressed them, treated them cruelly, curbed and molded their fine instincts by its materialism. In *Old Curiosity Shop*, when Little Nell goes to the races with the puppet show, she meets some gypsies, of whose children Dickens wrote: "The sunburnt faces of gypsy children, half naked though they be, suggest a drop of comfort. It is a pleasant thing to see that the sun has been there; to know that the air and light are on them every day; to feel that they *are* children, and lead children's lives; that if their pillows be damp, it is with the dews of Heaven, and not with tears; that the limbs of their girls are free, and that they are not crippled by distortions, imposing an unnatural and horrible penance upon their sex; that their lives are spent from day to day at least among the waving trees, and not in the midst of dreadful engines which make young children old before they know what childhood is, and give them the exhaustion and infirmity of age, without, like age, the privilege to die. God send that old nursery tales were true, and that gypsies stole such children by the score!"

Perhaps the best exposition of this theme of the innocence of the country versus the sinfulness of the city is expressed in *Barnaby Rudge*. The hero for which this book is named, being twenty-three years old, does not technically qualify as one of Dickens' youths. But he was an idiot with the mind of a child. Barnaby lives in the country happily, then comes to London where he is easily led to his downfall through participation in the Gordon Riots. In the country his enjoyments were "to walk, and run, and leap, till he was tired; then to lie down in the long grass, or by the growing corn, or in the shade of some tall tree, looking upward at the light clouds as they floated over the blue surface of the sky, and listening to the lark as she poured out her brilliant song. There were wild flowers to pluck . . . millions of living things to have an interest in, and lie in wait for, and clap hands and shout in memory of, when they had disappeared. . . . The world to him was full of happiness; in every tree, and plant, and flower, in every bird, and beast, and tiny insect . . . he had delight."

At the end of the book, after Barnaby has suffered in a prison cell and narrowly escaped being hung, his simple mind realizes that he must never again risk the corruption of the city, "neither to visit them, nor on any other pretence, no matter how full of promise and enjoyment, could he be persuaded to set foot in the streets: nor did he ever conquer this repugnance or look upon the town again."

Some happy children are found in four little stories that Dickens wrote for children, his only excursion into juvenile writing except for his *Child's History of England*, a tome which he dictated to his sister-in-law Georgiana in odd moments and which has little to do with children. The four children's stories were collectively titled *Holiday Romance* and first appeared in installments in an American magazine, "Our Young Folks," in 1868.

The four tales in *Holiday Romance* are light and whimsical fantasies that are supposedly written by children. The underlying theme is that children are in every way more knowledgeable about the important aspects of life than grown-ups, and the latter should be at some times indulged and at others punished for their eccentricities and lack of understanding. When he sent the manuscript to his American agent, Dickens wrote: "The writing seems to me so like children's that dull folks (on *any* side of *any* water) might perhaps rate it accordingly! . . . It made me laugh to that extent that my people here thought I was out of my wits, until I gave it to them to read, when they did likewise."

The first tale is "from the pen of William Tinkling, Esq." The esquire is aged eight and starts his story by saying that "Nettie Ashford is my bride. We were married in the right-hand closet in the corner of the dancing-school, where first we met, with a ring (a green one) from Wilkingwaters' toy-shop. *I* owed for it out of my pocket-money." The age of the bride is half past six. Next day Lieut. Col. Robin Redforth, aged nine, is wed to Alice Rainbird, aged seven. Master Tinkling's "peerless bride" was, "at the period of which we now treat, in captivity at Miss Grimmer's [school]. Drowvey and Grimmer is the partnership, and opinion is divided as to which is the greater beast. The lovely bride of the colonel was also immured in the dungeons of the same establishment. A vow was entered into, between the colonel and myself, that we would cut them out on the following Wednesday when walking two and two."

The colonel carefully plans the cutting-out expedition on paper. He will lead the attack while Master Tinkling waits behind a lamppost until he sees Miss Drowvey fall, at which he is to leap forward, seize his bride, and fight his way up the lane. But the signal for his participation never comes because, although the colonel attacks vigorously, waving his black banner (the colonel was a pirate before he was a colonel), Miss Drowvey refuses to fall: "The hated Drowvey in spectacles appeared to me to have muffled the colonel's head in his outlawed banner, and to be pitching into him with a parasol."

Next day at dancing school Master Tinkling's bride spurns him, handing him a paper on which is written the query, "Is my husband a cow?" The older colonel realizes that a syllable is missing; she means coward. Tinkling demands a trial by court-martial and a court is convened with some difficulty, "on account of the Emperor of France's aunt refusing to let him come out. He was to be the president. Ere yet we had appointed a substitute, he made his escape over the back-wall, and stood among us, a free monarch." By proving that a soldier's first duty is obedience and producing the colonel's written battle plan, which required him to wait behind the lamppost, Tinkling gains a "not guilty" verdict. The procession to celebrate his acquittal is interrupted by an unlooked-for event. "This was no other than the Emperor of France's aunt catching hold of his hair. The proceedings abruptly terminated, and the court tumultously dissolved."

Later, under a willow tree, prosaic reason is injected into

the proceedings by the distaff side of the group. " 'It's no use pretending any more, and we had better give it up,' said the bride of the colonel. 'If grown-up people *won't* do what they ought to do, and *will* put us out, what comes of our pretending?' " Miss Drowvey would not fall, the aunt of the Emperor of France brought a disgraceful end to the court-martial, and surely the grown-ups would not recognize their marriages. " 'If you knocked at the door and claimed me, after you were told to go away,' said the colonel's bride, 'you would only have your hair pulled, or your ears, or your nose. . . . And at your own homes, it would be just as bad. You would be sent to bed, or something equally undignified. Again, how would you support us?' "

The colonel proposes to support them "by rapine," but, asks his practical wife, " 'Suppose the grown-up people wouldn't be rapined?' " Then, said the colonel, they would have to pay the penalty in blood. " 'But suppose they should object,' retorted his bride, 'and wouldn't pay the penalty in blood or anything else?' " The colonel had no answer to this.

Master Tinkling's wife realizes that " 'The grown-up people are too strong for us. They make us ridiculous. Besides, they have changed the times.' " This latter fact was proved when there was no king present at the christening of Master Tinkling's baby brother, nor was there a queen nor even a fairy, good or bad. " 'We had an idea among us, I think,' said Alice, with a melancholy smile, 'we four, that Miss Grimmer would prove to be the wicked fairy, and would come in at the christening with her crutch-stick and give the child a bad gift. Was there anything of that sort? . . .

" 'It must be the grown-up people who have changed all this. *We* couldn't have changed it, if we had been so inclined, and we never should have been. Or perhaps Miss

Grimmer *is* a wicked fairy, after all, and won't act up to it because the grown-up people have persuaded her not to. Either way, they would make us ridiculous if we told them what we expected.' " The only solution, says Alice, is to wait and try to educate the grown-up people. " 'We will pretend that we are children; not that we are those grown-up people who won't help us out as they ought, and who understand us so badly. . . . We will wait—ever constant and true—till the times have got so changed that everything helps us out, and nothing makes us ridiculous, and the fairies have come back. We will wait—ever constant and true—till we are eighty, ninety, or one hundred. And then the fairies will send *us* children, and we will help them out, poor pretty little creatures, if they pretend ever so much.' "

The second tale is penned by seven-year-old Alice Rainbird. This concerns a king and a queen, who "had nineteen children, and were always having more. Seventeen of these children took care of the baby; and Alicia, the eldest, took care of them all. Their ages varied from seven years to seven months."

The king is quite unhappy because his job does not pay very well. Quarter day is a long way off and several of the dear children are growing out of their clothes. One day when he is going to the office in a melancholy mood he meets an old lady who, after inquiring whether he is the father of Princess Alicia, introduces herself as the Fairy Grandmarina. She tells the king that he is to give the Princess a portion of the salmon he has purchased for dinner and tell her to save the bone that she finds in it, and polish it till it shines like mother-of-pearl, and guard it carefully. When the king asks: " 'Is that all?' " she replies, " 'Don't catch people short, before they have done speaking. Just the way with you grown-up persons. You are always doing it.' "

The fairy continues to say that the bone will bring Alicia, only once, anything she wishes for, "PROVIDED SHE WISHES FOR IT AT THE RIGHT TIME." When the king starts to say, " 'Might I ask the reason?' " the fairy becomes absolutely furious. " *Will* you be good, sir?' " she exclaims, stamping her foot on the ground. " 'The reason for this, and the reason for that, indeed! You are always wanting the reason. No reason. There! Hoity toity me! I am sick of your grown-up reasons.' "

Immediately after this the queen becomes ill and is confined to her bed. "The Princess Alicia kept the seventeen young princes and princesses quiet, and dressed and undressed and danced the baby, and made the kettle boil, and heated the soup, and swept the hearth, and poured out the medicine, and nursed the queen, and did all that ever she could, and was as busy, busy, busy as busy could be."

Alicia is tempted to use the fishbone to make the queen well and consults "a most particularly confidential friend of hers, who was a duchess. People did suppose her to be a doll; but she was really a duchess, though nobody knew it except the princess. . . . People might have supposed that she never smiled and nodded; but she often did, though nobody knew it except the princess." Between them they decide that this is not the right time, that Alicia could cope with the situation and the queen would get well. There are other instances when she is tempted to use the bone. A snapping pug dog bites one of the princes and the baby falls under the grate, but the Princess Alicia handles these crises with effort and ingenuity and keeps the fishbone safe in the pocket of her apron. Then, one night, the king comes home very discouraged and the Princess asks:

" 'What is the matter, papa?'

" 'I am dreadfully poor, my child.'

" 'Have you no money at all, papa?'

" 'None, my child.'

" 'Is there no way of getting any, papa?'

" 'No way,' said the king. 'I have tried very hard, and I have tried all ways.'

"When she heard those last words, the Princess Alicia began to put her hand into the pocket where she kept the magic fishbone.

" 'Papa,' said she, 'when we have tried very hard, and tried all ways, we must have done our very, very best?'

" 'No doubt, Alicia.'

" 'When we have done our very, very best, papa, and that is not enough, then I think the right time must have come for asking help of others.' This was the very secret connected with the magic fishbone, which she had found out for herself from the good Fairy Grandmarina's words, and which she had so often whispered to her beautiful and fashionable friend, the duchess.

"So she took out of her pocket the magic fishbone, that had been dried and rubbed and polished till it shone like mother-of-pearl; and she gave it one little kiss, and wished it was quarter day. And immediately it *was* quarter day; and the king's quarter's salary came rattling down the chimney, and bounced into the middle of the floor."

Immediately thereafter the Fairy Grandmarina comes riding in "in a carriage and four (peacocks), with Mr. Pickle's boy up behind, dressed in silver and gold, with a cocked-hat, powdered hair, pink silk stockings, a jewelled cane, and a nosegay." After asking the king, "'Are you good?'" she says, "'I suppose you know the reason *now*, why my god-daughter here did not apply to the fishbone sooner?'" The king humbly admits that he does and the fairy tells him, "'Be good, then, and live happy ever afterward.'" She then waves her fan "and the seventeen young princes and princesses, no longer grown out of their clothes, came in, newly fitted out from top to toe, with tucks in everything to admit of its being let out." The fairy then whisks Alicia away in her carriage to pick up Prince Certainpersonio who "was sitting by himself, eating barley-sugar, and waiting to be ninety. When he saw the peacocks, followed by the carriage, coming in at the window, it immediately occurred to him that something uncommon was going to happen."

The fairy tells the royal couple that they are to marry and the ceremony is held forthwith with all of the couples' relatives and friends and the neighbors and the seventeen princes and princesses. Grandmarina gives a magnificent feast afterward at which she announces "to the king and queen that in future there would be eight quarter-days in every year, except in leap-year when there would be ten. She then turns to Certainpersonio and Alicia, and says: 'My dears, you will have thirty-five children, and they will all be good and beautiful. Seventeen of your children will be boys, and eighteen will be girls. The hair of the whole of your children will curl naturally. They will never have the measles, and will have recovered from the whooping cough before being born.'"

The third romance is the story of Lieut. Col. Robin Redforth, known throughout most of his career as Boldheart. At its opening, "We find him in command of a splendid schooner of one hundred guns loaded to the muzzle, ere yet he had had a party in honour of his tenth birthday." It seems that our hero, considering himself spited by a Latin-grammar master, demanded the satisfaction due from one man of honour to another. "Not getting it, he privately withdrew his haughty spirit from such low company, bought a second-hand pocket-pistol, folded up some sandwiches in a paper bag, made a bottle of Spanish liquorice-water, and entered on a career of valour."

Boldheart sails the China Seas, captures a whale single-handed, and takes many prizes. One morning a strange craft comes out of a harbor to challenge his craft, the "Beauty." The stranger hoists Roman colors. "Boldheart then perceived her to be the Latin-grammar master's bark. Such indeed she was, and had been tacking about the world in unavailing pursuit, from the time of his first taking to a roving life." After a tremendous fight Boldheart personally captures the Latin-grammar master. The crew wants to put him to death, for they feel that this is what a master who spites a boy deserves, but the noble Boldheart says nay. " 'Without taking your life,' said the captain, 'I must yet for ever deprive you of the power of spiting other boys. I shall turn you adrift in this boat. You will find in her two oars, a compass, a bottle of rum, a small cask of water, a piece of pork, a bag of biscuits, and my Latin grammar. Go! and spite the natives, if you can find any.' "

After a furious storm that lasts six weeks the "Beauty" is blown to a land of savages. When the captain and his men land they find the savages dancing around a large pot singing a chant which repeats the refrain: "Choo a choo a choo tooth. Muntch, muntch, Nycey!" They realize that this translates to, "For what we are going to receive, &," and see that the Latin master is in the pot, "with his head shaved, while two savages floured him, before putting him to the fire to be cooked!" The generous Boldheart resolves "that he should not be cooked, but should be allowed to remain raw, on two conditions, namely:

"1. That he should never, under any circumstances, presume to teach any boy anything more.

2. That, if taken back to England, he should pass his life in travelling to find out boys who wanted their exercises done, and should do their exercises for those boys for nothing, and never say a word about it."

They rescue the Latin master and take him with them as they sail on. When the ship is full of gold and jewels and elephant tusks and sandalwood, Boldheart turns her toward England. As they near their destination another ship comes to meet them flying a flag "which he instantly recognized as the flag from the mast in the back-garden at home." This vessel is the "Family," with Boldheart's parents, the majority of his aunts and uncles, and all of his cousins aboard. Boldheart sends a boat to find out whether his father's intentions are strictly honorable, and is advised that "the whole of these relations had expressed themselves in a becoming manner, and were anxious to embrace him and thank him for the glorious credit he had done them."

Boldheart takes them aboard and provides a great feast, which is marred only by the Latin master trying to communicate with the captain's parents with a view to giving up the "Beauty." The ingrate is hanged from the yardarm the next morning, "after having it impressively pointed out to him by Boldheart that this was what spiters came to."

The captain inquires of his mother about the young lady with whom he is in love. His mother tells him that the object of his affections "was then at school at Margate, for the benefit of sea-bathing . . . but that she feared the young lady's friends were still opposed to the union." Boldheart sails to Margate, resolving to bombard the town if necessary to gain his love, but when he lands and tells the trembling mayor, " 'help me to my bride, or be bombarded,' " that official agrees to cut the girl off from her bathing house so that Boldheart can capture her. All goes as planned and the loving couple are united and then married with great celebration. During this the mayor brings news that "government had sent down to know whether Capt. Boldheart, in acknowledgment of the great services he had done his country by being a pirate, would consent to be made a lieutenant colonel. For himself he would have spurned the worthless boon; but his bride wished it and he consented."

There was but one untoward incident. "It is painful to record (but such is human nature in some cousins) that Capt. Boldheart's unmannerly Cousin Tom was actually tied up to receive three dozen with a rope's end 'for cheekiness and making game,' when Capt. Boldheart's lady begged for him and he was spared. The "Beauty" then refitted, and the captain and his bride departed for the Indian Ocean to enjoy themselves for ever more."

The final tale, penned by Miss Nettie Ashford, aged half past six, concerns "a country, which I will show you when I get into maps, where the children have everything their own way. It is a most delightful country to live in. The grown-up people are obliged to obey the children, and are never allowed to sit up to supper, except on their birthdays. The children order them to make jam and jelly and marmalade, and tarts and pies and puddings, and all manner of pastry. If they say they won't, they are put in the corner till they do. They are sometimes allowed to have some; but when they

have some, they generally have powders given them afterwards."

One of the inhabitants of this country is a truly sweet
young creature by the name of Mrs. Orange, who is plagued
by her numerous family. "Her parents required a great deal
of looking after, and they had connections and companions
who were scarcely ever out of mischief. So Mrs. Orange said
to herself, 'I really cannot be troubled with these torments
any longer; I must put them all to school.' After taking off
her pinafore and dressing very nicely, Mrs. Orange picked up
her baby—'a very fine one, and real wax all over'—and called
on Mrs. Lemon, who kept a preparatory establishment, to
whom she said, " 'The truth, is ma'am, I have come to the
conclusion that my children,'—O, I forgot to say that they call
the grown-up people children in that country!—'that my
children are getting positively too much for me . . . Let me
see. Two parents, two intimate friends of theirs, one godfa-
ther, two godmothers, and an aunt. *Have* you as many as
eight vacancies?' "

Mrs. Lemon replies that she has just eight vacancies and
Mrs. Orange inquires about the terms, and the diet, and
whether corporal punishment is dispensed with. " 'Why, we
do occasionally shake,' said Mrs. Lemon, 'and we have
slapped. But only in extreme cases.' " They then go off to see
the establishment. In the schoolroom one boy is standing in a
corner and Mrs. Orange whispers to Mrs. Lemon to ask the
reason. " 'Come here, White,' said Mrs. Lemon, 'and tell this
lady what you have been doing.'

" 'Betting on horses,' said White sulkily.

" 'Are you sorry for it, you naughty child?' said Mrs.
Lemon.

" 'No,' said White. 'Sorry to lose, but shouldn't be sorry to win.'

" 'There's a vicious boy for you, ma'm,' said Mrs. Lemon.

" 'Go along with you, sir. This is Brown, Mrs. Orange. O, a sad case, Brown's! Never knows when he has had enough. Greedy. How is your gout, sir?'

" 'Bad,' said Brown.

" 'What else can you expect?' said Mrs. Lemon. 'Your stomach is the size of two. Go and take exercise directly.' "

Another unruly child is Mrs. Black who "can't be kept at home a single day together; always gadding about . . . from morning to night, and to morning again. . . .

" 'You must have a great deal of trouble with them, ma'am,' said Mrs. Orange.

" 'Ah, I have, indeed, ma'am!' said Mrs. Lemon. 'What with their tempers, what with their quarrels, what with their never knowing what's good for them, and what with their always wanting to domineer, deliver me from these unreasonable children!' "

After Mrs. Orange returns home Mrs. Alicumpaine calls upon her to say that she is giving a juvenile party and to ask Mr. and Mrs. Orange to help chaperone. Mr. Orange agrees reluctantly. He does not care for children and is tired from a hard day playing trap, bat and ball in the city, which "knocks a man up." The Oranges go to Mrs. Alicumpaine's where they are impressed with the refreshments that she has prepared for the guests. "Here's the supper for the darlings, ready laid in the room behind the folding-doors. Here's their little pickled salmon, I do declare! And here's their little salad, and their little roast beef and fowls, and their little pastry, and their wee, wee, wee champagne!"

When the children arrive many of them behave very badly,

as was to be expected. Some of them looked through quiz-
zing glasses at others and said: " 'Who are those? Don't
know them.' " The boys stand in groups and talk about newspapers or play Parliament instead of dancing. When Mrs. Alicumpaine makes them dance they won't smile but go round
and round the room in dismal twos. At first they will not
sing. Then, after drinking their wee, wee champagne, they
will not stop singing. "The girls were so ridiculously dressed,
too, that they were in rags before supper. How could the
boys help treading on their trains? And yet when their trains
were trodden on, they often showed temper again, and looked
as black, they did!"

At ten o'clock the children are fetched, by agreement, and
poor Mrs. Alicumpaine drops upon a sofa and says to Mrs.
Orange: " 'These children will be the death of me at last,
ma'am,—they will be indeed!' "

As Mr. and Mrs. Orange are walking home they pass Mrs.
Lemon's establishment and the mother looks up at the window
and wonders whether the precious children are asleep. Mr.
Orange replies that he does not care whether they are or not
and accuses his wife of doting on the youngsters. Mrs. Orange
admits this but wonders whether " 'our dear, good, kind Mrs.
Lemon would like them to stay the holidays with her.'

" 'If she was paid for it, I daresay she would,' said Mr.
Orange.

" 'I adore them, James,' said Mrs. Orange, 'but *suppose* we
pay her, then!'

"This was what brought that country to such perfection,
and made it such a delightful place to live in. The grown-up
people (that would be in other countries) soon left off being allowed any holidays after Mr. and Mrs. Orange tried the
experiment; and the children (that would be in other coun-

tries) kept them at school as long as ever they lived, and made them do whatever they were told."

Christmas was another of Dickens' crusades; or rather the proper celebration of Christmas as a time of joy in giving and sharing. He saw the season as a symbolic criticism of the relations that throughout the rest of the year exist between men and their fellow men, a time when generosity might overcome normal selfishness, a time when the spirit of brotherhood could be broadened to embrace a more active concern for the welfare of all mankind. Professor Johnson wrote that, to Dickens, Christmas was "a sign and an affirmation that men do not live by bread alone, that they do not live for barter and sale alone. No way of life is either true or rewarding that leaves out men's need of loving and of being loved." In a sense there was a connection in Dickens' thinking between the spirit of Christmas and the spirit of childhood, in that both placed spiritual above material values; both placed high value on love and an interplay between individuals as a necessity for a happier life.

Although Christmas has a special meaning to children, juvenile characters are incidental in Dickens' Christmas books, of which he wrote five, starting with *A Christmas Carol*, in 1843. *The Chimes* appeared in 1844, *The Cricket on the Hearth* in 1845, *The Battle of Life* in 1846, and *The Haunted Man* in 1847. With the exception of *A Christmas Carol* none of them were about Christmas, as such. The stories merely occurred at Christmas time. All except one were fantasies applied to the theme of the horror of man's inhumanity to man. They were essentially social criticisms rather than Christmas stories. *The Haunted Man* differs in that its major theme had its roots in Dickens' own past; it portrays a man who is made unhappy by his childhood memories. While there are incidental youthful characters in the other books—Meg Veck in *The Chimes* and the little blind Bertha Plummer in *Cricket on the Hearth*—juvenile characters play more significant roles in *The Haunted Man*.

This story concerns an outwardly successful man, Redlaw, who cannot escape from the wrongs and sufferings of his past. When he is visited by a specter he tells the shade: " 'I am he, neglected in my youth, and miserably poor, who strove and suffered, and still strove and suffered, until I hewed out knowledge from the mine where it was buried. . . . No mother's self-denying love, no father's counsel aided *me*. . . . My parents, at the best, were of that sort whose care soon ends, and whose duty is soon done; who cast their off-spring loose, early, as birds do theirs; and, if they do well, claim the credit; and, if ill, the pity.' "

Redlaw had a sister who died young. "Such glimpses of the light of home as I had ever known, had streamed from her. How young she was, how fair, how loving! I took her to the first poor roof that I was master of, and made it rich. She came into the darkness of my life, and made it bright." The parallels between Dickens' early life and Redlaw's are not exact or complete, but both involve rejective parents and Redlaw's sister is Dickens' sister-in-law, Maria Hogarth.

The ghost grants Redlaw's desire to lose his memory of wrong and sorrow, but with the gift goes the condition that he will pass it on to all with whom he comes in contact. Then Redlaw discovers that with the memory of unhappiness depart all tender memories as well, together with the softening influence that grief may bring. All those he meets become callous, surly, bitter, or brutal. An exception is a six-year-old boy who rushes into the room after the ghost has left. "A bundle of tatters, held together by a hand, in size and form

an infant's, but, in its greedy, desperate little clutch, a bad
old man's. A face rounded and smoothed by some half-dozen
years, but pinched and twisted by the experiences of a life.
Bright eyes, but not youthful. Naked feet, beautiful in their
childish delicacy—ugly in the blood and dirt that cracked
upon them. A baby savage, a young monster, a child who had
never been a child, a creature who might live to take the outward form of man, but who, within, would perish a mere
beast.

"Used, already, to be worried and hunted like a beast, the
boy crouched down as he was looked at, and looked back
again, and interposed his arm to ward off the expected blow.

" 'I'll bite,' he said, 'if you hit me!' "

Later, after Redlaw's gift has embittered several people,
the ghost visits him again and the man asks: " 'Why has this
child alone been proof against my influence, and why, why,
have I detected in its thoughts a terrible companionship with
mine?'

" 'This,' said the Phantom, pointing to the boy, 'is the last,
completest illustration of a human creature, utterly bereft of
such remembrances as you have yielded up. No softening
memory of sorrow, wrong, or trouble enters here, because
this wretched mortal from his birth has been abandoned to a
worse condition than the beasts, and has, within his knowledge, no one contrast, no humanizing touch, to make a grain
of such a memory spring up in his hardened breast. All
within this desolate creature is barren wilderness. All within
the man bereft of what you have resigned, is the same barren
wilderness. Woe to such a man! Woe, tenfold, to the nation
that shall count its monsters such as this, lying here, by hundreds and by thousands!' "

There are some happier children in *The Haunted Man* than

the ragged boy. These are the offspring of the Tetterbys. The Tetterby baby, Little Moloch, is a caricature that brings relief to what is otherwise a rather pallid story. Mr. Tetterby is a struggling newsdealer with a devoted wife and "any amount of small children you may please to name—at least it seemed so; they made, in that very limited sphere of action, such an imposing effect, in point of numbers.

"Of these small fry, two had, by some strong machinery, been got into bed in a corner, where they might have reposed snugly enough in the sleep of innocence, but for a constitutional propensity to keep awake, and also to scuffle in and out of bed. The immediate occasion of these predatory dashes at the waking world was the construction of an oyster-shell wall in a corner, by two other youths of tender age; on which fortification the two in bed made harassing descents (like those accursed Picts and Scots who beleaguer the early historical studies of most young Britons) and then withdrew to their own territory.

"In addition to the stir attendant on these inroads, and the retorts of the invaded, who pursued hotly, and made lunges at the bed-clothes under which the marauders took refuge, another little boy, in another little bed, contributed his mite of confusion to the family stock, by casting his boots upon the waters; in other words, by launching these and several small objects, inoffensive in themselves, though of a hard substance considered as missiles, at the disturbers of his repose —who were not slow to return these compliments."

In addition to the youngsters mentioned above there was another boy, Johnny, "the biggest there, but still little—was tottering to and fro, bent on one side, and considerably affected in his knees by the weight of a large baby, which he was supposed, by a fiction that obtains sometimes in sanguine families, to be hushing to sleep." Caring for the baby was Johnny's responsibility and the mammoth infant was a heavy cross for a small boy to bear. "It was a very Moloch of a baby, on whose insatiate altar the whole existence of this particular young brother was offered up a daily sacrifice. Its personality may be said to have consisted in its never being quiet, in any one place, for five consecutive minutes, and never going to sleep when required. 'Tetterby's baby' was as well known in the neighborhood as the postman or the pot-boy. It roved from door-step to door-step, in the arms of little Johnny Tetterby, and lagged heavily at the rear of troops of juveniles who followed the Tumblers or the Monkey, and came up, all on one side, a little too late for everything that was attractive, from Monday morning until Saturday night. Wherever childhood congregated to play, there was little Moloch making Johnny fag and toil. Wherever Johnny desired to stay, little Moloch became fractious, and would not remain. Whenever Johnny wanted to go out, Moloch was asleep, and must be watched. Whenever Johnny wanted to stay at home, Moloch was awake, and must be taken out. Yet Johnny was verily persuaded that it was a faultless baby, without its peer in the realm of England, and was quite content to catch meek glimpses of things in general from behind its skirts, or over its limp flapping bonnet, and to go staggering about with it like a very little porter with a very large parcel, which was not directed to anybody, and could never be delivered anywhere."

The Tetterbys, when first introduced, are a happy family despite their poverty. Mrs. Tetterby brings home from the cookshop a pork knucklebone on which there is not much meat but there is "no stint of seasoning, and that is an accessory dreamily suggesting pork, and pleasantly cheating the sense of taste . . . so upon the whole, there was the flavour of a middle-sized pig." When his parents ate, Johnny "received his rations on bread, lest he should, in a flush of gravy, trickle any on the baby. He was required, for similar reasons, to keep his pudding, when not on active service, in his pocket." The feast is irresistible to the smaller Tetterbys who are in bed and "though professing to slumber peacefully, crawled out when unseen by their parents, and silently appealed to their brothers for any gastronomic token of fraternal affection. They, not hard of heart, presenting scraps on return, it resulted that a party of light skirmishers in night-gowns were careering about the parlour all through supper, which harassed Mr. Tetterby exceedingly, and once or twice imposed upon him the necessity of a charge, before which these guerilla troops retired in all directions and in great confusion."

Very early one morning, after his gift from the ghost, Redlaw passes through the Tetterby's room on his way to see a lodger upstairs. This brief contact immediately changes the Tetterby family. Mr. Tetterby sees that his wife is fat and aging, she sees that he is common-looking, stooped, and bald. They start to bicker and regret their marriage and the children. As to these, "The tempers of the little Tetterbys had sadly changed with a few hours. . . . They were fighting now, not only for the soap and water, but even for the breakfast which was yet in perspective. The hand of every little Tetterby was against the other little Tetterbys; and even Johnny's hand—the patient, much enduring, and devoted Johnny—rose against the baby! Yes. Mrs. Tetterby, going to the door by a mere accident, saw him viciously pick out a weak place in the suit of armour where a slap would tell, and slap that blessed child."

Johnny had reason, other than Redlaw's visit, for his brutal conduct. The baby was teething. "It was a peculiarity of this baby to be always cutting teeth. Whether they never came, or whether they came and went away again, is not in evidence; but it had certainly cut enough, on the showing of Mrs. Tetterby, to make a handsome dental provision for the sign of the Bull and Mouth. . . . Mrs. Tetterby always said it was coming through, and then the child would be herself; and still it never did come through, and the child continued to be somebody else." Johnny resolves that he is going to be a soldier, " 'There ain't no babies in the army.' "

At the end of the story the ghost's gift is canceled and all those who have become embittered by contact with Redlaw are made whole when he meets them again. On a later visit to the Tetterbys, "He saw the children throng about her, and caress her . . . he heard the ringing of their laughter, and their merry voices; he saw their bright faces, clustering round him like flowers; he witnessed the renewed contentment and affection of their parents; he breathed the simple air of their poor home, restored to its tranquillity."

The greatest of all Dickens' Christmas stories is, of course, *A Christmas Carol*—there are many who maintain that it is the greatest Christmas story ever written, second only to the Nativity story in Matthew. The reading of it aloud was a Christmas Eve tradition in hundreds of thousands of homes for almost a century before the modern means of communication came into existence. Thanks to radio and television it is today probably Dickens' best-known work. Oldsters remember when no Christmas was complete without hearing Lionel Barrymore play Scrooge on radio, and youngsters today have a choice of two motion picture versions of the tale which vie for the tube before Christmas.

A Christmas Carol is a fantasy that illustrates how Christ-

mas can and should bring love and brotherhood into the life
of man. Secondarily, it is a criticism and an exposé of the callous attitude of the English mercantile system toward the
poor and underprivileged. Its principal character, Scrooge,
is a man who has grown old in selfishness and monetary
greed. His life is limited to cashboxes, ledgers, and bills of
sale; there is no place in it for sentiment, tenderness, or generosity. Writes Dickens: "Nobody ever stopped him in the
street to say, with gladsome looks, 'My dear Scrooge, how
are you? when will you come to see me?' No beggars im-
plored him to bestow a trifle, no children asked him what it
was o'clock, no man or woman ever once in all his life inquired the way to such and such a place, of Scrooge. Even
the blindmen's dogs appeared to know him; and when they
saw him coming on, would tug their owners into doorways
and up courts; and then would wag their tails as though they
said, 'No eye at all is better than an evil eye, dark master!' "
When his nephew drops into his counting house on Christmas Eve to wish him a merry Christmas, the old man replies:
"Bah!—humbug."

That night Scrooge is visited by the ghost of his deceased
partner, Marlow, a shade which trails a long chain comprised
of cashboxes, keys, padlocks, and heavy purses wrought in
steel. The ghost tells him that he is suffering in eternity for
the wrongs he committed during his lifetime by his lack of
concern for others and that Scrooge will suffer the same fate
unless he heeds the three spirits that will visit him that night.
The three spirits, the Ghost of Christmas Past, the Ghost of
Christmas Present, and the Ghost of Christmas Future, work
the redemption of Scrooge and make him realize, for his own
happiness, the necessity of a concern for others, by taking
him to view Christmas from his childhood to his grave.

The first spirit takes him back to see himself, a lonely boy reading in school when others have gone on a holiday. Then his sister comes to get him and joyfully tells him that she has come to bring him home where, " 'We're to be together all the Christmas long, and have the merriest time in all the world.' " In another scene he sees himself as the apprentice to Old Fessiwig, who sends him to put the shutters up early so that there may be a joyful office party. After other views of his youth, Scrooge is returned to his bed to await the second spirit.

The Ghost of Christmas Present takes him to see how others are celebrating Christmas and what Scrooge is missing. Before leaving, the ghost discloses two children to the old misanthrope; another presentation of the doomed children that are so often found in Dickens' work. "From the foldings of its robe, it brought two children; wretched, abject, frightful, hideous, miserable. They knelt down at its feet, and clung upon the outside of its garment. . . . They were a boy and a girl. Yellow, meagre, ragged, scowling, wolfish; but prostrate, too, in their humility. Where graceful youth should have filled their features out, and touched them with its freshest tints, a stale and shrivelled hand, like that of age, had pinched and twisted them, and pulled them into shreds. Where angels might have sat enthroned, devils lurked, and glared out menacing. No change, no degradation, no perversion of humanity, in any grade, through all the mysteries of wonderful creation, has monsters half so horrible and dread. . . .

" 'They are Man's,' said the Spirit, looking down upon them. 'And they cling to me, appealing from their fathers. This boy is Ignorance. This girl is Want. Beware them both, and all of their degree, but most of all beware this boy, for on his brow I see that written which is Doom, unless the writing be erased.' "

This same ghost takes Scrooge to see the Cratchit's celebrating Christmas. Bob Cratchit is Scrooge's clerk. Earlier in the story the old man has reluctantly given Bob the day off, although he feels Christmas is a "poor excuse for picking a man's pocket every twenty-fifth of December," by being paid for no work. He cannot understand how Bob has anything to be merry about on his miserable stipend of fifteen shillings a week.

The Christmas dinner at the Cratchit's is the happiest family scene to be found in all of Dickens, and one of the most moving and compelling presentations of the true Christmas spirit ever written. The little cripple, Tiny Tim, who is introduced here, made such an impression when the book was first published that a charitable organization was formed called The Tiny Tim Guild to relieve the plight of poor crippled children in England. The Christmas dinner scene is surely worth quoting at length to conclude this presentation of children and youth in the works of Dickens.

"Then up rose Mrs. Cratchit, Cratchit's wife, dressed out but poorly in a twice-turned gown, but brave in ribbons, which are cheap and make a goodly show for sixpence; and she laid the cloth, assisted by Belinda Cratchit, second of her daughters, also brave in ribbons; while Master Peter Cratchit plunged a fork into the saucepan of potatoes, and getting the corners of his monstrous shirt-collar (Bob's private property, conferred upon his son and heir in honour of the day) into his mouth, rejoiced to find himself so gallantly attired, and yearned to show his linen in the fashionable Parks. And now two smaller Cratchits, boy and girl, came tearing in, screaming that outside the baker's they had smelt the goose, and known it for their own; and basking in luxurious thoughts of sage-and-onion, these young Cratchits danced about the table, and exalted Master Peter Cratchit to the skies, while he (not proud, although his collar nearly choked him) blew the fire, until the slow potatoes, bubbling up, knocked loudly at the saucepan-lid to be let out and peeled.

" 'What has ever got your precious father then,' said Mrs. Cratchit. 'And your brother, Tiny Tim; and Martha warn't as late last Christmas Day by half-an-hour!'

" 'Here's Martha, mother!' said a girl, appearing as she spoke.

" 'Here's Martha, mother!' cried the two young Cratchits. 'Hurrah! There's *such* a goose, Martha!'

" 'Why, bless your heart alive, my dear, how late you are!' said Mrs. Cratchit, kissing her a dozen times, and taking off her shawl and bonnet for her, with officious zeal.

" 'We'd a deal of work to finish up last night,' replied the girl, 'and had to clear away this morning, mother!'

" 'Well! Never mind so long as you are come,' said Mrs. Cratchit. 'Sit ye down before the fire, my dear, and have a warm, Lord bless ye!'

" 'No, no! There's father coming,' cried the two young Cratchits, who were everywhere at once. 'Hide, Martha, hide!'

"So Martha hid herself, and in came little Bob, the father, with at least three feet of comforter exclusive of the fringe, hanging down before him; and his thread-bare clothes darned up and brushed, to look seasonable; and Tiny Tim upon his shoulder. Alas for Tiny Tim, he bore a little crutch, and had his limbs supported by an iron frame!

" 'Why, where's our Martha?' cried Bob Cratchit looking round.

" 'Not coming,' said Mrs. Cratchit.

" 'Not coming!' said Bob, with a sudden declension in his high spirits; for he had been Tim's blood horse all the way from church, and had come home rampant. 'Not coming upon Christmas Day!'

"Martha didn't like to see him disappointed, if it were only in joke; so she came out prematurely from behind the closet door, and ran into his arms, while the two young Cratchits hustled Tiny Tim, and bore him off into the wash-house, that he might hear the pudding singing in the copper.

" 'And how did little Tim behave?' asked Mrs. Cratchit, when she had rallied Bob on his credulity and Bob had hugged his daughter to his heart's content.

" 'As good as gold,' said Bob, 'and better. Somehow he gets thoughtful sitting by himself so much, and thinks the strangest things you ever heard. He told me, coming home, that he hoped the people saw him in the church, because he was a cripple, and it might be pleasant to them to remember, upon Christmas Day, who made lame beggars walk and blind men see.'

"Bob's voice was tremulous when he told them this, and trembled more when he said that Tiny Tim was growing strong and hearty.

"His active little crutch was heard upon the floor, and back came Tiny Tim before another word was spoken, escorted by his brother and sister to his stool beside the fire; and while Bob, turning up his cuffs—as if, poor fellow, they were capable of being made more shabby—compounded some hot mixture in a jug with gin and lemons, and stirred it round and round and put it on the hob to simmer, Master Peter and the two ubiquitous young Cratchits went to fetch the goose, with which they soon returned in high procession.

"Such a bustle ensued that you might have thought a goose the rarest of all birds; a feathered phenomenon, to which a black swan was a matter of course: and in truth it was something very like it in that house. Mrs. Cratchit made the gravy (ready beforehand in a little saucepan) hissing hot; Master Peter mashed the potatoes with incredible vigour; Miss Belinda sweetened up the apple-sauce; Martha dusted the hot plates; Bob took Tiny Tim beside him in a tiny corner at the table; the two young Cratchits set chairs for everybody, not forgetting themselves, and mounting guard upon their posts, crammed spoons into their mouths, lest they should shriek for goose before their turn came to be helped. At last the dishes were set on, and grace was said. It was succeeded by a breathless pause, as Mrs. Cratchit, looking slowly all along the carving-knife, prepared to plunge it in the breast; but when she did, and when the long expected gush of stuffing issued forth, one murmur of delight arose all round the board, and even Tiny Tim, excited by the two young Cratchits, beat on the table with the handle of his knife, and feebly cried Hurrah!

"There never was such a goose. Bob said he didn't believe there ever was such a goose cooked. Its tenderness and flavour, size and cheapness, were the themes of universal admiration. Eked out by the apple-sauce and mashed potatoes, it was a sufficient dinner for the whole family; indeed, as Mrs. Cratchit said with great delight (surveying one small atom of a bone upon the dish), they hadn't ate it all at last! Yet every one had had enough, and the youngest Cratchits in particular were steeped in sage and onion to the eyebrows! But now, the plates being changed by Miss Belinda, Mrs. Cratchit left the room alone—too nervous to bear witnesses—to take the pudding up, and bring it in.

"Suppose it should not be done enough! Suppose it should break in turning out! Suppose somebody should have got over the wall of the back-yard, and stolen it, while they were merry with the goose: a supposition at which the two young Cratchits became livid! All sorts of horrors were supposed.

"Hallo! A great deal of steam! The pudding was out of the copper. A smell like a washing-day! That was the cloth. A smell like an eating-house and a pastry cook's next door to each other, with a laundress's next door to that! That was the pudding. In half a minute Mrs. Cratchit entered, flushed, but smiling proudly, with the pudding, like a speckled cannon-ball, so hard and firm, blazing in half of half-a-quartern of ignited brandy, and bedight with Christmas holly stuck into the top.

"Oh, a wonderful pudding! Bob Cratchit said, and calmly too, that he regarded it as the greatest success achieved by Mrs. Cratchit since their marriage. Mrs. Cratchit said that now the weight was off her mind, she would confess she had had her doubts about the quantity of flour. Everybody had something to say about it, but nobody said or thought it was at all a small pudding for a large family. It would have been flat heresy to do so. Any Cratchit would have blushed to hint at such a thing.

"At last the dinner was all done, the cloth was cleared, the hearth swept, and the fire made up. The compound in the jug being tasted and considered perfect, apples and oranges were put upon the table, and a shovel-full of chestnuts on the fire. Then all the Cratchit family drew round the hearth, in what Bob Cratchit called a circle, meaning half a one; and at Bob Cratchit's elbow stood the family display of glass: two tumblers and a custard-cup without a handle.

"These held the hot stuff from the jug, however, as well as

golden goblets would have done; and Bob served it out with beaming looks, while the chestnuts on the fire sputtered and crackled noisily. Then Bob proposed:

" 'A Merry Christmas to us all, my dears. God bless us!'
"Which all the family re-echoed."

And then occurs the most memorable line in all of Dickens' writing—perhaps one of the most memorable lines in all of English literature—spoken by one of Dickens' vast multitude of youthful characters.

" 'God bless us every one!' said Tiny Tim, the last of all."

INDEX

INDEX